THE IDEA OF THE
CATHOLIC UNIVERSITY

THE IDEA OF THE
CATHOLIC UNIVERSITY

Proceedings from the 30th Annual Convention
of the Fellowship of Catholic Scholars

September 28-30, 2007
Washington, D.C.

Edited by Kenneth D. Whitehead

**Library of Congress
Cataloging-in-Publication Data**

(Has been applied for but is not available at time of publication.)

Distribution:

UNIVERSITY OF SCRANTON PRESS
Chicago Distribution Center
11030 S. Langley
Chicago, IL 60628

CONTENTS

Editor's Note

Kenneth D. Whitehead

SINCE ITS BEGINNINGS, it has been the custom of the Fellowship of Catholic Scholars to collect the speeches, responses, remarks, and other contributions delivered at the Fellowship's annual conventions and make them available in the form of a paperback book to the entire membership of the association. Usually only one-tenth to one-fifth of the membership actually attends the annual conventions, but it has also consistently been the Fellowship's custom to invite scholars and speakers of proven and even distinguished merit to make significant contributions to the subject chosen for the theme of each annual convention. These papers constitute an important part of the work of the Fellowship, in fact, and are generally well worth reproducing and sharing with those members unable to attend a given convention as well as with the public at large. Over the years these published "proceedings" of the Fellowship conventions add up to important additions to our knowledge on a variety of subjects of contemporary Catholic interest; they also contribute importantly to the defense of Catholic truth at the time and place in which we currently live not always immediately disposed to appreciate or credit Catholic truth.

No convention of the Fellowship of Catholic Scholars takes place without the express permission of the bishop of the diocese in which the convention is being held, and, indeed, almost always, with his participation.

The theme of the Fellowship's 30th annual convention held in Washington, D.C., on September 28-30, 2007, was: "The Idea of the Catholic University for the Twenty-first Century" (shortened for the title of this book to *The Idea of the Catholic University*). The program committee, under the chairmanship of Fordham's Father Joseph W. Koterski, S.J., was able to put together a first-class program on this subject. We are now pleased to be able to make available in book form the important contributions that were made to this subject at the convention by the invited speakers, panelists, and respondents.

Program Chairman's Introduction

Reverend Joseph W. Koterski, S.J.

FOR THE 30TH ANNUAL CONVENTION of the Fellowship of Catholic Scholars, borrowing a line from Cardinal Newman, we chose as our theme: "The Idea of the Catholic University for the Twenty-First Century."

Our keynote speaker for this meeting was Archbishop Donald W. Wuerl of Washington, who also celebrated Mass for the membership on Saturday morning, September 29, 2007, prior to delivering his keynote address later in the day. The title of this keynote address was based on the convention's own theme, namely: "Elements of a Catholic University for the Twenty-First Century."

The convention opened on Friday, September 28, with addresses by two fine Newman scholars. Professor John Crosby of the Franciscan University of Steubenville, reflecting on the role of the Catholic university, especially as regards the Church's engagement with contemporary culture, focused not only on Newman's *The Idea of a University,* but also on his *Essay on the Development of Christian Doctrine.* Professor Karl Schmude of Campion College in Australia, a long-time member of the Fellowship from down under, compared the figure of St. Edmund Campion to that of Cardinal Newman, while considering the relationship of religious truth to the question of intellectual freedom.

The convention offered a number of panels on contemporary educational issues. On Friday evening, Dr. Melanie Morey and Father John Piderit, S.J., authors of the recent study, *Catholic Higher Education: A Culture in Crisis* (New York:

Oxford University Press, 2006), offered to the convention the results of their study of various models for Catholic higher education. Father David M. O'Connell, C.M., president of the Catholic University of America, then presented a response to the Morey-Piderit offering.

On Saturday morning, September 29, another panel on Catholic Studies programs at Catholic universities, introduced by Robert F. Gotcher of the Sacred Heart School of Theology in Wisconsin, featured discussions by Sister Paula Jean Miller, F.S.E., of the University of St. Thomas in Houston, Texas, and Professor John Cavadini of the University of Notre Dame in South Bend, Indiana. On the important topic of the engagement of the Catholic University with the secular culture, on Saturday afternoon, Professor Christopher Wolfe of Marquette University in Milwaukee, and Professor Michael Aeschliman of Boston University, both covered significant aspects of this important topic.

On Sunday morning, September 30, Monsignor Stuart W. Swetland, now at St. Mary's Seminary in Emmitsburg, Maryland, although formerly he was the chaplain at the Newman Center at the University of Illinois, and Professor Robert L. Wilken of the University of Virginia, both discussed aspects of the subject of Catholic education on secular campuses. The Cardinal Wright Award recipient for 2007 was Father Thomas G. Weinandy, O.F.M. Cap., a previous keynoter at the 2006 FCS convention, who is currently serving as executive director of the Secretariat for Doctrine and Pastoral Practice of the U.S. Conference of Catholic Bishops (USCCB).

As always, the program for the 2007 FCS convention provided much food for thought along with much good Catholic fellowship as these various subjects were considered and discussed.

Reverend Joseph W. Koterski, S.J., is a member of the Philosophy Department at Fordham University in the Bronx, New York, where he has taught since his priestly ordination in 1992. He currently serves as the Editor-in-Chief of the *International Philosophical Quarterly* and as chaplain in the Queen's Court Residential College for Freshmen. He teaches courses on natural law ethics and medieval philosophy, and has produced lecture courses on "Aristotle's Ethics" and on "Natural Law and Human Nature" for the Teaching Company. Among his recent publications are: *The Two Wings of Catholic Thought: Essays on* Fides et Ratio (2003) and *Karl Jaspers on the Philosophy of History and the History of Philosophy* (2003). A new monograph of his, *An Introduction to Medieval Philosophy: Some Basic Concepts*, is scheduled for publication in 2008.

KEYNOTE ADDREESS

Elements of a Catholic University for the Twenty-First Century

Most Reverend Donald W. Wuerl, S.T.D.
Archbishop of Washington

It is an honor and pleasure for me to have this opportunity to speak to this 30th Annual Convention of the Fellowship of Catholic Scholars held here in the nation's capital where I am privileged to serve as bishop. In a particular way I want to thank Father Joseph Koterski, S.J., for his gracious invitation to be with all of you today to discuss the important topic of the idea of a Catholic university in the 21st century.

In speaking of the role of a Catholic university and, in particular, in highlighting elements of a Catholic university that need to be underlined in our day and as we move into this new century, I think it is important to point out that much of what we would envision as elements of an authentically Catholic university have already been experienced in the life of the Church. We are well served, I believe, by looking at the long history of Catholic institutions of higher education to see what enduring and essential elements of the concept of the Catholic university need to be revisited today.

In the introduction to the apostolic constitution on Catholic universities, *Ex Corde Ecclesiae*, Pope John Paul II reminded all of us that "born from the heart of the Church, a Catholic university is located in that course of tradition which may be traced back to the very origin of the university as an institution." "By vocation," Pope John Paul II continued, "the *Universitas Magistrorum et Scholarum* is

1

dedicated to research, to teaching, and to education of students who freely associate with their teachers in a common love of knowledge." Here, interestingly enough, while these words ring as relevant to our contemporary situation, the pope is not citing a recent directive from the Congregation for Catholic Education or even from the Congregation for the Doctrine of Faith, but rather a letter of Pope Alexander IV to the University of Paris in 1255 A.D.

As we begin these reflections, I would like to touch on the origin and purpose of Catholic institutions of higher learning and later distill some elements that would continue to serve us into the next century.

Beginnings and Hallmarks of Catholic Universities

The beginnings of Catholic colleges and universities in the United States are found in the desire of Catholics to provide an education that would be rooted in Catholic teaching and demonstrative of those truths and values taught by the Catholic Church.

Historically, we can trace the beginnings of some Catholic colleges, and later universities, to the works of religious communities of women and religious communities of men.

Other colleges were started by groups of lay women and lay men in collaboration with the local bishop. The board of trustees in one way or another was directly or indirectly related to the bishop.

Another, although less frequently used, form in the United States for the foundation of a college or university was its establishment by a diocesan bishop or by a group of bishops.

The purpose of all of these institutions was, of course, to provide an academically excellent education in the context of the Catholic faith and in the environment of Catholic life. Hence, the role of Catholic theology, the celebration of the liturgy, and the school's relationship to the bishop as head of the local Church were seen as hallmarks of Catholic identity.

Today and into the future the same hallmarks are necessary. A Catholic university should be an academic center where the faith permeates the culture. The liturgical celebration of the faith should be an integral part of the school's program and routine. The institution's communion with the Church should be clearly seen in how the university relates to the bishop as head of the local Church.

Today, however, there is an additional element that we need to highlight. A Catholic college or university should reflect its identity by its involvement as an institution in the presentation of issues and questions challenging our culture and society. This point we will return to later.

The first and most obvious beneficiaries of a Catholic university are its students. The Church also benefits from having as a part of its lived experience the vital intellectual and academic center that is a university. In dioceses all over this country there are examples of how the Church has benefited because there is in her midst a college or university that shares the mission of those who claim discipleship in Christ.

The wider community also benefits from the presence of a Catholic university. Clearly, the pluralism represented by an alternative program of education can only enrich the community. A Catholic university has the unique capacity to deal with and emphasize the spiritual dimension of human life. Revelation, religious conviction, and faith enable the student and professor to carry our understanding of human existence beyond the natural and physically verifiable into the spiritual dimension needed for full and complete human life.

One of the distinct benefits of a Catholic college or university is its ability to act as a bridge between the wider community and the experiences of students in that wider community with the Church as the faith community of so many of the same students. Just as in the growing experience at every stage in life there is the need for our faith to engage the world around us and our own ability to enter into that active initiative, so on the level of a Catholic campus there should be an awareness that the faith itself must be woven into the fabric of the university if it is truly going to help the student engage the culture from a uniquely Catholic perspective.

Because each college or university by its very nature is accustomed to relating to all types of communities that impact on the nature of the university, the role of faith and the ministry of the Church should be readily welcomed into the fabric of a Catholic university.

A university, Catholic or secular, does not carry out its mission alone. No university exists in a vacuum. A university is a part of the society and the community in which it lives as well as the more confined community that it serves.

The interrelation of a university with all of the various institutions and communities in which it lives and moves and has its being brings us to a vast complex of relationships far beyond the bounds of the campus.

Universities relate with that world known as the academic community. This can take the form of the accreditation of a university by those associations which not only monitor universities but enforce specific standards.

The *mandatum* required by the application of the Apostolic Constitution *Ex Corde Ecclesiae* is an ecclesial manifestation of the academically acceptable declaration of certification. The *mandatum* is the credential that affirms in a verifiable manner that the Catholic professor who teaches ecclesial sciences does so in communion with the Church—in the communion of the Church.

Internal to the university are its many schools and departments that pursue the excellence of the discipline in their particular care. Yet even within each of the sciences there is a responsibility to the lived practice of that science—a lived practice outside the academic community and off of the campus. For example, internal to the mechanism of a law school are, in fact, the decisions of the Supreme Court which determine jurisprudence for this nation. Such determinations are not external to the study of law but, in fact, are an integral part of a good law school. The intervention of the Supreme Court and its decisions are not an intrusion by an outside, extraneous force but the articulation of an intrinsic aspect of the American development of law.

The study of medicine includes an understanding of the role of the Federal Drug Administration and the limits imposed on the use of certain unapproved medicines. Even in areas of the sciences such as engineering, there is the interrelationship with the corporate world where the practical effects of engineering find their lived acceptance or rejection. Often this takes the form of grants and funding of approved programs.

Relationship with the Church

Because a Catholic university undertakes to teach, among other things, the faith of the Catholic Church, and to advance that faith by a more profound understanding of its implications and applications in our day, the university necessarily relates to the rest of the Church and specifically to the hierarchy.

The Magisterium is the office in the Church that has the care of revelation and the Church's teaching. It accredits or affirms that what is taught is recognizable as Catholic teaching. In this sense, the Bishop is never "outside" any part of the believing community. Within the development of Catholic theology, the Magisterium exercises an intrinsic function. The Magisterium or teaching office in the Church is never extrinsic or unrelated to the Church's understanding of her faith. *"Fides quaerens intellectum,"* by definition, is an ecclesial action.

In the introduction to *Ex Corde Ecclesiae*, Pope John Paul II reminded us that "a Catholic university's privileged task is 'to unite intrinsically by intellectual effort two orders of reality that too frequently tend to be placed in opposition as though they were antithetical: the search for truth and the certainty of already knowing the fountain of truth'" (Pope John Paul II, Discourse to the *Institut Catholique de Paris*, 1980, 1).

A Catholic college or university, by very definition, must be a place of higher education where the voice of the great Catholic tradition rooted in God's revelation and expounded in the lived tradition of the Church impacts the vision, life, and witness of the school. In this sense, the richness of Catholic theology can engage the secular culture with its many technological and scientific advances in a way that the light of the wisdom of God is brought to bear on the issues of the day.

One of the major cornerstones of Catholic "identity" is the communal character of faith. The Church is not simply a collection of believers who think and act the same way. The Church, the Body of Christ, is united in the theological virtues of faith, hope and love. Within the Church the Spirit is recognized to move simultaneously on at least three levels: the study of faith and morals by *theologians* (whose authority derives not from their office but from their skills of scholarship and the arguments they put forth to support their positions); the spiritual or almost intuitive grasp of the wholeness of the faith by the *faithful*; and the authoritative judgment of the *bishops*, who have the pastoral care of the Church as their ministry.

The three realities are not the same and do not function in an identical way. All three are distinct yet complementary. Each can act as a reference point or corrective for the others in the process of understanding our faith. While the three operate within the same community of faith they also have as their common purpose the building up of the Church. Nonetheless, they are distinct realities.

The Church as a Functioning Community of Faith

One of the most helpful images emphasized by the Second Vatican Council is that of "the people of God" on a pilgrimage. This image assists us in understanding that we are a united people with a common heritage, purpose and goal. It also helps us to understand that despite our goal, we have not yet arrived at its achievement. Our journey proceeds with the assistance of many elements. Among the shared experiences of our community life are prayer, reflection, study, discussion, and the experience of the apostolate. All of these elements complement each other and contribute to the common experience of unity.

In a similar way, the community itself, the bishops and the theologians, must work together in the common enterprise. Rooted in a common baptismal origin, each member's growth in faith enriches the entire body. In this way, both theologians and bishops retain their membership within the community of the baptized despite the additional role they play. It is, therefore, from within the community that they exercise their role.

There has long been with the tradition of the Church an understanding of the intuition of the people of God. Even in the very critical early centuries of the Church, the great dogmas of faith were very much the product of the community at prayer. This notion of *lex orandi, lex credendi* has contributed clarity and stability to the growth of the faith.

The dwelling of the Holy Spirit within the community does not convey some secret wisdom to a few. Nor does it consist in private revelations and small group miracles. It is meant for the community in the tradition of the sages, judges. And prophets of old. It is the reflection of the faithful on the public revelation and deposit of faith synonymous with the apostolic Church. Both the theologians and the bishops should be attuned to this wisdom alive in the faith community of God's people, of which both theologians and bishops are a part.

Theology attempts to respond to changing human realities in a way that reflects new insights. Theology seeks to integrate human sciences with the Church's tradition of wisdom and the absolute claims of revelation. Theologians exercise a ministry of service for the good of the whole Church, and the spiritual well-being of all the people.

Yet by the very fact that theology has as its starting point revelation and the judgment concerning the truth of that revelation, theological science is different from every other type of science. Intrinsic to theology is both the objective truth of revelation and the normative guidance of the Magisterium, or teaching office, within the Church.

In the model of academic freedom used historically in the Church, freedom of discussion and investigation was but one component in a much wider process that led to judgment about the authenticity of a teaching.

In the ecclesial model of academic freedom, the propositions of theologians do not automatically translate into authentic Church teaching. Involved in the wider process is the recognition of the role of the Holy Spirit which manifests itself in the "*Sensus Fidei*" of the faithful and final approbation by the bishops.

In this model, the whole Church participates in the process according to the gifts and ministries with which the Spirit blesses the Church. Hence, we come to consider the role of the college of bishops. They too, through a common baptism share a place within the community of believers. Yet it was Christ who chose from among the baptized, certain members to fulfill a unique office ordered towards unity. Jesus said, "You are Peter, and upon this rock I will build my Church." Thus tied to the special role given to Peter, and rooted in the special sacrament of Ordination, bishops receive a unique mission within the community. The Catholic theological tradition includes as intrinsic to the process of theological development, the voice of the teaching office (Magisterium). The exercise of the office of bishop is not external to or extraneous to the Church's self-understanding, but is a service that is vital and essential part of the process (cf. *Lumen Gentium*, 25).

On the major issues of our doctrinal and moral lives there cannot exist alternative or opposing truths, or else the very unity of the community of faith will be threatened. There can be a process of development of doctrine but there cannot be mutually exclusive and contradictory teaching claiming to bind together the faith community. Ultimate responsibility for making these judgments rests with the bishops who succeed the college of apostles.

In highlighting the role of Catholic theology on the campus of a Catholic college or university, I have tried to do so in a way that emphasizes how permeating such Catholic thought should be. The student coming on to the campus should recognize that there is an institutional commitment to Catholic faith, thought, and values. Thus students find themselves embraced in a context that speaks of a specific vision of life and encourages them to a way of life that is demonstrative of Catholic faith and morals.

Institutional Identity

But there is another dimension to Catholic identity on campus. This I touched on earlier. Not only should Catholic teaching be reflected in the appropriate classroom and students be expected to live a way of life reflective of and inspired by Catholic teaching, but the institution itself should speak to and engage the wider community in issues from a Catholic perspective. This is perhaps the single most challenging and, I think, important dimension of a Catholic college or university going into the future. Its Catholic identity should be the identity of the institution itself and not simply reflected in some of its faculty and student body. To name a college or university a Catholic institution of higher learning is to label it an intellectual and academic partner of an ecclesial vision of life that is rooted in Jesus Christ, articulated in his Gospel, and manifested in his Church.

It should not be at all surprising that a Catholic university would speak to technological, scientific, and life issues today from a distinctly Catholic perspective. In this way, in the great cultural issues and national debates that touch on matters of the natural moral law and human dignity, there would be an institutional voice at the college/ university level reflective of the intellectual tradition out of which the institution comes and for which it should be a supportive voice of the teaching of the Church.

A number of years ago when I served in the Pittsburgh diocese, I invited the three Catholic institutions of higher learning there, Duquesne University, Carlow University, and LaRoche College, to do something for the Year of the Eucharist that would show an institutional appreciation of this doctrine of the faith in a way that would be faithful both to the Church's teaching and to the unique academic institution that is a college or university. The results were varied in their manifestation and positive in approach. While each university chose a different format, what resulted were symposia, lecture series, and seminars on all three campuses, presenting a deeper and academically qualified and intellectually profound discussion of the Church's understanding of the great gift of the Eucharist.

One could envision in this century Catholic colleges and universities making an institutional contribution to some of the issues of the national debate that often lack a perspective reflective of the intellectual heritage of a university rooted in the Gospel. One could envision a series of symposia, seminars, workshops and lectures to present Catholic teaching on areas such as beginning and end of life issues, the understanding of marriage in the natural moral order, and the social justice teaching found in a continuum of encyclicals from *Rerum Novarum* through to *God Is Love*.

The Catholic university provides the academic home for the engagement of faith and reason and the ongoing effort to shed greater light on the human condition. In addition to offering an environment that respects revealed truth and the moral order rooted in creation, a Catholic university should at the same time be an institutional voice in our world for the very values that faith holds up for us. Its institutional witness, therefore, can be a formative influence in our society.

As we reflect on the role of a Catholic university today, we need to address its understanding of the relationship to truth that both faith and reason have, and the importance of the living, teaching tradition of the Church that articulates today the experience of the apostles. At the same time, we must consider how the university can engage our culture with the faith as an institution itself, committed to the integration of the light of faith and the light of reason and the perennial search for truth. Not only should we see no opposition between the search for truth and the certainty of already knowing the font of truth, we should not see opposition between our identity as a Catholic institution of higher learning and our ability as such to address the issues of the day.

Conclusion

In concluding these remarks, I want to return to the significance of authentic Catholic teaching on the campus of Catholic colleges and universities.

Catholics continue to live on the campuses of our nation and through the world—and here they should grow strong in wisdom and grace. The Catholic community of faith embraces the world of academia and in fact continues to sponsor its local manifestations throughout the world. The Catholic on campus stands as a unique individual, free yet formed by faith.

The Catholic university of tomorrow should be for its students and for the Church what a Catholic institution of higher learning has been envisioned to be in the tradition of the Church. The name "Catholic" calls it to be an academic community whose vision of life derives from the Gospel of Christ. As a manifestation of the life and mission of the Church, a Catholic university should bring a voice of values and speak out of a vision of faith to the wider world around it. In this way, its privileged claim to grow out of the heart of the Church is translated into an intellectual and moral blessing—a blessing so sorely needed by our society today.

Every member of the Catholic Church, whether on campus or not, is truly free but never alone. Even on a campus a member of the Catholic Church is part of the community—a community of believers, teachers, and bishops, all born of the same baptismal bath and all committed to the same goal. But each has different gifts. All of those gifts are at our disposal for our journey of faith—a journey of faith on which we never walk alone!

Archbishop Donald W. Wuerl is the sixth archbishop of Washington, installed on June 22, 2006. He is thus the spiritual leader of some 580,000 Catholics in 140 parishes in Washington, D.C., and five Maryland counties.

Archbishop Wuerl is the chairman of the Committee on Catechesis of the United States Conference of Catholic Bishops (USCCB) and the chairman of the board of the National Catholic Education Association (NCEA). He was heavily involved in the development of the *United States Catholic Catechism for Adults*, published in 2006. He also serves on other national and international bodies, and is an elected member of the council for the Vatican office for the Synod of Bishops. He is the chairman of the board of directors of the Basilica of the National Shrine of the Immaculate Conception, the chancellor of the Catholic University of America, and the former chairman of the National Catholic Bioethics Center's board of directors.

Archbishop Wuerl was born in Pittsburgh on November 12, 1940, was ordained to the priesthood in 1966, and became a bishop in 1986. He served as bishop of his native Pittsburgh for eighteen years before coming to Washington. He has earned graduate degrees from the Catholic University of America and the Gregorian University in Rome, as well as a doctorate in theology from the University of St. Thomas in Rome. He is the author or co-author of a number of books in his own right, and once served as secretary to the late Cardinal John J. Wright, prefect of the Congregation for the Clergy in Rome (and himself a former bishop of Pittsburgh), for whom the principal award made by the Fellowship of Catholic Scholars is named. Archbishop Wuerl is himself a paid perpetual member of the Fellowship, and has participated in several FCS conventions.

Cardinal Newman
and the Idea of a University

How the Gospel Encounters
the Culture in the Catholic University:
Some Lessons from
John Henry Newman

John F. Crosby

IN *EX CORDE ECCLESIAE*, John Paul the Great teaches that "a Catholic university, aware that human culture is open to revelation and transcendence, is also a primary and privileged place for a fruitful dialogue between the Gospel and culture"(43). My question is: how would the great John Henry Newman explain this dialogue between the Gospel and culture? Newman was himself a university man, the founder of a university, and the author of the classic on university education, *The Idea of a University*. And Newman resourcefully engaged the culture that he found around him in 19th century Europe. In fact, as a Catholic he wanted to engage it more actively than his religious superiors allowed. So what does he say about the encounter of the Gospel with that surrounding culture that does not base itself on the Gospel? The Church has been enriched by Newman's thought at so many levels: surely he has something to say about how Christian intellectuals, and Christian universities, should conduct themselves in the encounter with the world of secular intellectual culture.

It is natural to turn first to his *The Idea of a University* and to look there for an answer to our question. In this work Newman masterfully characterizes the distinctly intellectual virtues of a liberally educated person. He introduces his ideal of the "imperial intellect," of which he says that this intellect "never views any part of the extended subject-matter of knowledge without recollecting that it is but a part, or without the associations which spring from this recollection. It makes everything thing lead in some sort to everything else; it would communicate the image of the whole to every separate portion...giving them one definite meaning."[1]

We all need to learn from Newman this sense of the whole of truth, and how we can take our bearings within the whole without being omniscient. But these rich lessons of *The Idea of a University* do not, it seems to me, directly touch our question of how the Gospel encounters the surrounding culture in the setting of a university. What speaks more to our question is Newman's great seminal study, his *Essay on the Development of Christian Doctrine*. Though Newman in that book is not directly addressing the work of a Catholic university, it will not be difficult to adapt some of his ideas to our question about how this work is to be conducted.

In the essay on doctrinal development Newman compares the original Christian idea to a seed. Now a seed cannot be kept in a dry and safe place, but must be planted in the earth and exposed to hot and cold and wet and dry, and it and must come into contact with nutrients in the soil. Only in this way can the seed germinate and the plant unfold and eventually grow, as the case may be, into a massive tree.[2] Now the Christian idea, in the vision of Newman, is planted in the soil of history. In the interchange with its historical environment it unfolds, manifesting aspects of itself that were only virtually present in the seed. Newman appropriates for his understanding of this unfolding of Christian doctrine the parable of "the grain of mustard-seed...which indeed is the least of all seeds, but when it is grown it is the greatest among herbs, and becometh a tree." This soil of history, in which the Christian seed is planted, includes what we were calling above the surrounding culture; and the interchange of the evangelical seed with its historical soil includes that encounter of the Gospel with the culture that is our subject.

Here is the idea in Newman's own words:

But whatever be the risk of corruption from intercourse with the world around, such a risk must be encountered if a great idea is duly to be understood, and much more if it is to be fully exhibited. It is elicited and expanded by trial and battles into perfection and supremacy. Nor does it...remain truer to itself, and with a better claim to be considered one and the same, though externally protected from vicissitude and change. It is indeed sometimes said that the stream is clearest near the spring. Whatever use may fairly be made of this image, it does not apply to the history of a philosophy or belief, which on the contrary is more equable, and purer, and stronger, when its bed has become deep, and broad, and full.[3]

We know from our individual experience how we need the encounter with other minds in order to know what we really think, and in order to deepen our meaning. Our own inner life becomes sterile if deprived of the lively interchange with others who can challenge us. It is in something like this way, Newman says, that the Church needs its cultural environment in order to develop its self-understanding.

It may be objected that in the case of the Gospel we have not a human philosophy but something that descends from above, and that surely it is not subject to the law of gradual unfolding over time. The objection is that what Newman is formulating in his essay is a law for earthly and human ideas, and that this succession of aspects slowly revealed over time, ill befits a revelation that comes to us directly from God. Newman answers that if the boy Jesus, divine person though he was, could "grow in wisdom and stature," why should not His Church grow in wisdom through the ages? He finds nothing more mysterious or more surprising in the fact of the Gospel being subject to an historical development than he finds in the fact of the God-man being subject to spiritual growth. Both facts just serve to show the radicality of the incarnation.[4] In fact, Newman thinks that in a sense the need for an unfolding in time is greater with a divine revelation than with some merely human idea. For the plentitude of a divine revelation is far less able than some human philosophy to be adequately displayed in a single historical moment; the greater the plentitude, the more elaborate and prolonged the process that unfolds and articulates it.

Let us think with Newman a little more closely about this

encounter between the Gospel and the culture. It clearly has a negative moment. "No one doctrine can be named which starts complete at first, and gains nothing afterwards from the investigations of faith and the attacks of heresy."[5] We who live and work in Catholic universities experience this all the time; we come to understand our faith better when we are attacked and have to give an account of it. We would have continued taking our faith for granted, but false teachings, distorted models for living, inverted value hierarchies force us to think more closely about it and to understand it more deeply. The struggle may be arduous, but we gain in the process a development of our Christian self-understanding.

But what interests me even more in Newman's essay on doctrinal development is his idea that the Christian encounter with the culture is not limited to this moment of rejecting error. He says: "The idea never was that throve and lasted, yet, like mathematical truth, incorporated nothing from external sources. So far from the fact of such incorporation implying corruption, as is sometimes supposed, development is a process of incorporation."[6] Later in the essay on doctrinal development, Newman distinguishes between authentic developments and corruptions of doctrine, and he proposes seven criteria for making the distinction; his third criterion is what he calls the "power of assimilation" proper to authentic developments. "Assimilation" expresses as well as "incorporation" this moment in the encounter with the culture that surpasses the moment of identifying error and evil in the culture.

Now as soon as we talk about a task of assimilating elements from the surrounding culture, Christian intellectuals get worried about the danger of being assimilated by what is in the end foreign to the Gospel. They can point to plenty of examples of being assimilated. Many allege, for example, that Christianity has been excessively "Hellenized" in the encounter with Greek philosophy, and that authentic Christianity can be retrieved only through a work of "de-Hellenization," or de-assimilation. They say that our task is to preserve the Christian message in its purity and that we are sure to dilute it if we start assimilating elements from the surrounding culture. Better to begin and end our engagement with the culture, they say, with that negative moment that we were just discussing.

Newman does not agree. Though he had a strong sense of

the inner unity of Christian revelation, and of all that is contrary to this unity, he nevertheless goes very far in affirming the power of assimilation that is proper to Christian revelation. He thinks that much that at first glance looks like a foreign addition and hence a corruption, is in fact a successful assimilation, an assimilation that stands in the service of a deepened Christian self-understanding. Newman gives a powerful expression to his view in a study published a few years before the essay on doctrinal development. In this study he was reviewing a history of Christianity written by an Anglican historian named Milman. He found in Milman a principle that he paraphrased as follows: "That nothing belongs to the Gospel but what originated in it; and that whatever, professing to belong to it, is found in anterior or collateral systems, may be put out of it as a foreign element."[7] Milman is just the kind of writer who would think of the influence of Greek philosophy in Christianity as a suspicious "Hellenization" of Christianity. Here is a really memorable passage from Newman's review of Milman (a passage that was much admired by Henri deLubac):

> Now, the phenomenon, admitted on all hands, is this:—that a great portion of what is generally received as Christian truth, is in its rudiments or in its separate parts to be found in heathen philosophies and religions. For instance, the doctrine of a Trinity is found both in the East and in the West; so is the ceremony of washing; so is the rite of sacrifice. The doctrine of the Divine Word is Platonic; the doctrine of the Incarnation is Indian; of a divine kingdom is Judaic; of Angels and demons is Magian; the connexion of sin with the body is Gnostic...a sacerdotal order is Egyptian; the idea of a new birth is Chinese and Eleusinian; belief in sacramental virtue is Pythagorean; and honours to the dead are a polytheism. Such is the general nature of the fact before us; Mr. Milman argues from it,—"These things are in heathenism, therefore they are not Christian:" we, on the contrary, prefer to say, "these things are in Christianity, therefore they are not heathen." That is, we prefer to say, and we think that Scripture bears us out in saying, that from the beginning the Moral Governor of the world has scattered the seeds of truth far and wide over its extent; that these have variously taken root, and grown up as in the

wilderness, wild plants indeed but living; and hence that, as the inferior animals have tokens of an immaterial principle in them, yet have not souls, so the philosophies and religions of men have their life in certain true ideas, though they are not directly divine. What man is amid the brute creation, such is the Church among the schools of the world; and as Adam gave names to the animals about him, so has the Church from the first looked round upon the earth, noting and visiting the doctrines she found there...And wherever she went, in trouble or in triumph, still she was a living spirit, the mind and voice of the Most High; "sitting in the midst of the doctors, both hearing them and asking them questions;" claiming to herself what they said rightly, correcting their errors, supplying their defects, completing their beginnings, expanding their surmises, and thus gradually by means of them enlarging the range and refining the sense of her own teaching.

Newman concludes this passage with an extremely strong statement about the place of incorporation and assimilation in this encounter of the Gospel with surrounding cultures:

So far then from her creed being of doubtful credit because it resembles foreign theologies, we even hold that one special way in which Providence has imparted divine knowledge to us has been by enabling her to draw and collect it together out of the world, and, in this sense, as in others, to suck the milk of the Gentiles...[8]

I can't resist quoting a few more sentences from the next page; this is after all the central idea that I want to get out of Newman for our reflection on the Catholic university in the new century.

The distinction between these two theories is broad and obvious. The advocates of the one imply that Revelation was a single, entire, solitary act, or nearly so, introducing a certain message; whereas we, who maintain the other, consider that Divine teaching has been in fact..."at sundry times and in divers manners," various, complex, progressive, and supplemental of itself. We consider the Christian doctrine, when analyzed, to appear, like the human frame,

"fearfully and wonderfully made;" but they think it some
one tenet or certain principles given out at one time in
their fullness, without gradual enlargement before Christ's
coming or elucidation afterwards…They are ever hunting
for a fabulous primitive simplicity; we repose in Catholic
fullness.[9]

You see what I want to get out of Newman for our work
of building up our universities. When as Christian intellectuals we
encounter the surrounding secular culture, we not only have the task
of repelling error, but also the task of appropriation, incorporation,
assimilation, in a word, the task of "sucking the milk of the Gentiles"
and of enlarging the "Catholic fullness" that we inherit. I see this lesson
from Newman as distinctly encouraging for us, because it reminds us
that in the encounter with the culture we face not only danger but also
opportunity.

I might pause here for a moment to mention that Newman
has a great ally in Benedict XVI. Recall his defense of reason in
Regensburg. Benedict said that rather than coercing each other, we
should reason with each other, but that our ability to live by reason
depends on our understanding of God. We have to think of God
as *logos* or reason if we are going to commit ourselves to a life of
reason. And we Christians, the pope said, derive our understanding
of God as *logos* from Greek philosophy. The Christian commitment
to reason, which he said distinguishes the Christian God from Allah,
is, then, the fruit of a certain assimilation, a certain "Hellenization"
of the Christian proclamation. Perhaps the pope would be willing
to use Newman's language and to say that the early Church did not
try to hold fast to a "fabulous primitive simplicity," but was ready to
encounter the surrounding Greek culture in such a way as to grow in
"Catholic fullness."

But I sense that some committed Christian intellectuals will
still hold out against the idea that I am taking from Newman.[10] Some
may think that there is an unreal optimism in this idea of "sucking
the milk of the Gentiles," at least when the "Gentiles" are not Plato
and Aristotle but are the leading figures in our post-Christian secular
culture. I take this concern seriously, and will now try to find a voice
for it in a well-known sermon that Newman preached in 1873 on the
occasion of the dedication of a seminary. Then I will try to articulate

Newman's response to the concern. In that sermon, speaking in a prophetic tone of voice, he said:

> I think that the trials which lie before us are such as would appal and make dizzy even such courageous hearts as St. Athanasius, St. Gregory I, or St. Gregory VII. And they would confess that, dark as the prospect of their own day was to them severally, ours has a darkness different in kind from any that has been before it.[11]

Newman then explains the new kind of darkness that he foresees: "Christianity has never yet had experience of a world simply irreligious." And you may say: "That is exactly the point. When the surrounding culture is 'simply irreligious,'"[12] then it will surely offer little that is fit to be incorporated into Christian self-understanding. When Newman speaks about incorporation and assimilation he is thinking of the earlier age of the world when people were still religiously awakened and felt strong religious aspirations. But Newman would have certainly not continued to speak so hopefully about incorporation,you say, if he had lived to experience a culture that has fallen into the darkness of being "simply irreligious." He would have agreed that in our day the task is simply to refute error and to keep revelation free from corruption and compromise. This is what one may say on hearing these somber words of Newman from 1873.

But I do not think that Newman, even in his darkest prophetic moments, would have fallen back to this primarily defensive strategy. He would continue to say to us even today that the Church "'sits in the midst of the doctors, both hearing them and asking them questions'... and thus gradually by means of them enlarging the range and refining the sense of her own teaching." Let us take a strictly empirical approach. Can we discern any processes going on in our time that Newman would recognize as processes of Christian assimilation and incorporation in his sense? Can we settle the question of whether assimilation is possible for us even today by showing that it is a present reality? Now if we are going to answer in this empirical way, then we need examples. Here is one.

Romano Guardini has written about a new understanding of the "solidity" of the natural world that emerges in modern science.[13] He says that pre-modern Christians too often invested the natural world with so much symbolic religious significance that the reality proper to the natural world was not appreciated. Modern science, says Guardini, takes this reality very seriously and experiences it very strongly. When Christians think about this new experience of a certain autonomy of natural things and natural processes, they realize that it is not necessarily a godless way of experiencing the world, but that it can be incorporated into the Christian understanding of the dignity of creation. Guardini says that the Christian God creates not just shadows and puppets but independent beings; the generosity of the creator gives rise to a creation that has its own being and is subject to its own laws. And so it was never right from a Christian point of view to dissolve natural things into religious symbols.

Perhaps we can even say that certain very significant sentences in paragraph 36 of *Gaudium et Spes* on "the autonomy of earthly affairs" represent a Christian assimilation of the de-mythologized and de-numinized sense of the natural world that characterizes the modern sensibility. Note well that I am not saying that the Church has to turn to modern science in order to learn about the dignity of creation. No, she possesses a divine revelation about Creator and creation. But she does not receive this revelation in its fullness from the beginning; and she is enabled to articulate it and to understand it more deeply when she finds herself challenged by a new experience of the solidity of the natural world, even though that experience arose outside of the Church and was at first often coupled with antagonism to the Church. She will, of course, have to reject certain interpretations of this solidity of the natural world, such as the interpretation according to which the finite world is impenetrable to God, that is, is so autonomous as to eliminate the possibility of God being actively present in the midst of it. But she rejects this interpretation for the sake of salvaging something that is worthy of being incorporated into her self-understanding, for the sake of salvaging something that resonates with and serves to elicit her own faith about creation and the Creator.

It follows from this example that the assimilation and appropriation of which Newman speaks really is possible in relation to our secular culture; it must be possible because it is actually happening. If space permitted, I think I could show how Newman himself actively participated in a significant process of assimilation and appropriation: I could show that Newman's Christian personalism[14] did not derive only from established Catholic sources but also from Newman assimilating elements from the larger intellectual culture of his age, and this despite the growing darkness of his age. I could also show that John Paul II took very seriously the modern "discovery of subjectivity" and was thereby enabled to achieve the depth that he achieved in his thinking about the human person. The moral governor of the world is evidently not being prevented, not even in the midst of our own special trials at the beginning of the 21st century, from "scattering the seeds of truth" in the world, as Newman put it. And so the appropriation of which Newman speaks continues to be possible to us.

Now what I want to say is that this work of appropriation can and should take place in a particularly conscious and critical way in Catholic universities. Of course, it is a vaster work of appropriation than Newman discusses, since it is not limited to the development doctrine; it also comprises ethos, artistic sensibility, model-persons, patterns of life. The task of engaging the surrounding culture on all these levels is a task that is entrusted in a particular way to the Catholic university, for it engages all the energies and gifts of the Catholic university. There is a work here of discriminating, of accepting and rejecting, of transforming that is best carried out in the setting of a Catholic university.

I conclude with what Newman teaches about the kind of commitment to truth that we have to have if we are to be capable of this encounter with the surrounding culture. Without this commitment to truth we cannot stand our ground, we cannot resist *being assimilated.* In one of the most memorable passages in the *Essay on the Development of Christian Doctrine*, Newman gives a description both of the deficient commitment to truth and of the full-bodied commitment to truth. The description is found in the section on the power of assimilation that is proper to genuine developments. Those who are still be holding out against Newman may finally come around when they see how much he thinks is required of those who venture to assimilate things from the culture. Here is the deficient commitment to truth, which has no power of assimilation.

> That truth and falsehood in religion are but matter of opin-
> ion; that one doctrine is as good as another; that the Gov-
> ernor of the world does not intend that we should gain the
> truth; that there is no truth; that we are not more acceptable

to God by believing this than by believing that; that no one is answerable for his opinions; that they are a matter of necessity or accident; that it is enough if we sincerely hold what we profess; that our merit lies in seeking, not in possessing; that it is a duty to follow what seems to us true, without a fear lest it should not be true...that we may take up and lay down opinions at pleasure; that belief belongs to the mere intellect, not to the heart also; that we may safely trust to ourselves in matters of Faith, and need no other guide,—this is the principle of philosophies and heresies, which is very weakness.[15]

If we encounter the culture with this mentality, we are sure to be taken over by the culture, absorbed by it; we are sure to be vulnerable to its darkness and to be harmed by its poison. We will at best accumulate ideas from the culture in a syncretistic way, but will do no real work of assimilation and incorporation. Here now is how Newman unforgettably characterizes the ardent commitment to truth, which alone has a real power of assimilation.

That there is a truth then; that there is one truth; that religious error is in itself of an immoral nature; that its maintainers, unless involuntarily such, are guilty in maintaining it; that it is to be dreaded; that the search for truth is not the gratification of curiosity; that its attainment has nothing of the excitement of a discovery; that the mind is below truth, not above it, and is bound, not to descant upon it, but to venerate it; that truth and falsehood are set before us for the trial of our hearts; that our choice is an awful giving forth of lots on which salvation or rejection is inscribed; that "before all things it is necessary to hold the Catholic faith;" that "he that would be saved must thus think," and not otherwise; that, "if thou criest after knowledge, and liftest up thy voice for understanding, if thou seekest her as silver, and searchest for her as for hid treasure, then shalt thou understand the fear of the Lord, and find the knowledge of God,"—this is the dogmatical principle, which has strength.[16]

Newman proceeds to say that this "dogmatical principle" expresses the same ardent commitment to truth that was lived out by the martyrs. It takes nothing less than this commitment for us to be strong enough to devour the rods of the Egyptian magicians, as Newman says, strong enough to absorb from the culture what is congenial to revelation while rejecting what is corrosive of it. This tells us something about the kind of intense and serious Catholic life that should exist at the heart of a Catholic university. But as our Catholic life becomes more serious and more committed, we university people do not just witness against the surrounding culture, but we are also empowered to "suck its milk" and so to enlarge what Newman calls our "Catholic fullness."

Professor John F. Crosby has been a professor of philosophy at the Franciscan University of Steubenville since 1990. Prior to that he taught at the University of Dallas and at the International Academy of Philosophy. He received his doctorate in philosophy from the University of Salzburg in 1970. He has published many philosophical articles and translations as well as two books: *Personalist Papers* (2004) and *The Selfhood of the Human Person* (1996). Among his special academic interests, he lists the thought of Dietrich von Hildebrand and John Henry Cardinal Newman.

Endnotes

[1]Newman, *The Idea of a University,* Discourse 6, "Knowledge Viewed in Relation
[2]Learning," Section 6.
[3]Quoted by Newman, *An Essay on the Development of Christian Doctrine* (Notre Dame IN: University of Notre Dame Press, 1989), 73.
[4]*Ibid.,* 39-40.
[5]Cf. *Ibid.,* 57.
[6]*Ibid.,* 68.
[7]*Ibid.,* 186.
[8]Newman, *Essays Critical and Historical*, vol. 2 (London: Longmans, Green, and Co., 1907), 230.
[9]*Ibid.,* 231-232.
[10]*Ibid.,* 233.
[11]See the interesting discussion of some of them in Robert Benne's article in *First Things*, "The Neo-Augustinian Temptation," Vol. 81 (March, 1998), 14-16.
[12]Newman, "The Infidelity of the Future," *Catholic Sermons of Cardinal Newman* (London: Burns and Oates, 1957), 121.
[13]*Ibid.,* 123.
[14]In the following, I make use of Guardini, *Welt und Person* (Wuerzburg, 1952), 24-36.
[15]Cf. My study, "John Henry Newman on Personal Influence," in my *Personalist Papers* (Washington DC: Catholic University of America Press, 2004), 221-242. Newman, Essay on the Development of Christian Doctrine, op. cit., 357-358.
[16]*Ibid.,* 357.

Campion and Newman: The Peter and Paul of Catholic Higher Education

Karl G. Schmude

EDMUND CAMPION AND JOHN HENRY NEWMAN: both can stake a large claim to importance in the idea of a Catholic university, Newman very plainly and recognizably so, his classic work, *The Idea of a University*, forming the indicative title of this year's Fellowship conference. Yet Campion, too, embodies a vital part of the Catholic educational tradition, even if his contribution is less amply documented and less widely known.

Let me begin by sketching a picture of these two remarkable men. They are foundational figures of Catholic higher education: the "twin towers," as it were, of the Catholic university. They were born three centuries apart, Campion in the 16th century, amid the religious and political turmoil of the English Reformation, and Newman in the 19th century, a period of great religious and intellectual controversy. I imagine each of them, characteristically, in a cell. Campion at first occupied the secret cell where he was found and captured, the special hiding place in English Catholic houses used by Campion and other priests, during this period of persecution, in the event of a sudden raid by the authorities; and finally, the prison cell to which he was consigned in the Tower of London—a cell understatedly known as the "Little Ease" because of its cramped shape that prevented its occupant from standing or lying comfortably.

From these cells in Elizabethan England, Campion, still a relatively young man, radiated energy and inspiration; it was the energy of a scholar and lecturer, a man of learning, the inspiration of an apostle and martyr, a man of faith. I imagine him in his pain, not only physical pain, having been tortured on the rack and now facing the horror of being hanged, drawn and quartered, but also the mental and emotional anguish of a priest trying to shepherd his people in the midst of persecution.

John Henry Newman, too, I picture in a cell. In his case, it is a scholar's cell, with Newman composing tirelessly at his desk, producing so many memorable works. In these writings, especially his private letters and diaries, I sense his pain as well—the pain of isolation, both religious and cultural, and of frustration of his talents, especially during the last half-century of his life as a Catholic. Newman lived to a formidable old age—he was almost 90 when he died—by contrast with the relative youth of Campion at his martyrdom.

In each case, the cell they inhabited was a symbol of their religious fidelity. It was a consecrated place in which they lived out their vocation of witness to the truth. We can, perhaps, see it as, in Campion's case, a consecration of the martyr's heart, and in Newman's case, a consecration of the teacher's mind.

In each case, again, I like to imagine them in their cells as they lived out their last days, and to wonder if they called to mind the mission they had carried out to exalt the truth in their time, and to build the "idea" of a university for our time. Indeed, all time.

In this paper I will be striving to do two things: first, to compare the contributions of Campion and Newman to an understanding of Catholic higher learning, both philosophically and institutionally; and secondly, to consider the ways in which Campion and Newman epitomized the Catholic intellectual vocation, and carried out in the university sphere the leadership exerted more broadly in the life of the Church by Saints Peter and Paul.

Campion and Newman were both born in London, but they were quintessentially men of Oxford. Each was the outstanding Oxford figure of his time. Campion was a person of precocious brilliance. Several years after he left Oxford, he was described by Lord Cecil, an architect of the English Reformation, as "one of the diamonds of England."[1] He was appointed a Fellow of St John's College, Oxford, at the age of 17, and he attracted a personal following, and exercised an intellectual influence, that was not rivaled for another three centuries—until John Henry Newman did the same, attending Trinity College, Oxford, as an undergraduate, and becoming a Fellow of Oriel

College at the age of 21. Newman called Oxford "the most religious university in the world,"[2] and the institution played a decisive part in forming the religious and intellectual sensibilities of Campion in the 16th century and of Newman in the 19th century.

Speaking of the members of the Oxford Movement, Newman said that Catholics did not influence their conversion to Catholicism. "Oxford," he said, "made us Catholics."[3] Campion and Newman each delivered memorable sermons in the University Church of St Mary the Virgin in Oxford. Campion did so indirectly when his work of apologetics called *Ten Reasons* was secretly printed and left on the pews of the church, arousing the hostility of the authorities and causing a massive search for him—said to be the largest manhunt at that time in English history—which culminated in his capture and execution.

Newman also spoke at the University Church, only he did so in person, and frequently, when he served as Vicar (1828-1843) during his Anglican years. Both Campion and Newman loved Oxford, and the Oxford experience shaped their philosophy of education and their devotion to the university as an institution.[4] Each tried to establish a Catholic university, and each was unsuccessful at the time. These efforts both took place in Ireland. Campion sought to revive a university that had lapsed, a papal foundation of the 14th century, which was later to materialize as Trinity College, Dublin. Newman was deeply engaged in the founding of the Catholic University of Ireland; and while it, too, did not really flourish in Newman's lifetime, it inspired the lectures which he delivered in Dublin and formed the foundation of his famous work, *The Idea of a University*.

What was Newman's "idea'" of a university? It was at once a positive concept, shaped and sharpened by negative forces. The positive content was the study of various subjects or branches of knowledge—commonly called the "liberal arts"—so as to enlarge and cultivate the mind and produce an integrated understanding of knowledge and truth. In this Newman stressed the compatibility—even more, the necessary interdependence—of religion and learning, of faith and reason, of revelation and the imagination, as forming the unity and universality of truth.[5]

At the same time, Newman's concept of a liberal education—the education that befits a free man, and particularly a free *lay* man, since Newman had a deep desire to foster an educated *laity*[6]—is heightened by the defects and distortions of higher education, which have remained up to our own time, and indeed have intensified; especially the utilitarian view which confuses education with vocational training, and the clerical attitude which mistakes a university for a seminary.[7]

Campion, too, had a deep sense of a liberal education, though, by comparison with Newman, only fragments survive to illustrate his outlook. After leaving Oxford, he spent some time in Ireland, and his writings of that period reflect his rich understanding of university culture, combining habits of mind and demeanor that constitute the ideal student.[8] A discourse he wrote in Ireland entitled *The Academic Man*, was described by the English Jesuit, Father C.C. Martindale, as anticipating Newman's *Idea of a University*.[9] Campion stressed, for example, the blending of morals and manners with the cultivation of learning; the importance of piety and humility as well as healthy habits of study and recreation. In Ireland, he offered this advice to a student:

> . . .[B]ury yourself in your books, complete your course .
> . . keep your mind on the stretch . . . strive for the prizes
> which you deserve . . .Only persevere, do not degenerate
> from what you are, nor suffer the keen eye of your mind to
> grow dark and rusty.[10]

In an oration he delivered in France, at the seminary of Douai, not long afterwards, he was even more explicit on what was required of a student. The ideal student must keep his mind subtle, his memory active, his voice resonant; he should cultivate his pronunciation; his recreations are to be painting, playing the lute and writing music; and he should be devoted to languages, Latin, Greek and his own English tongue, in which he must compose verses and epigrams; by his 16th year, he must be able to produce Greek iambic verse![11]

When Campion later arrived in the city of Prague, after his ordination as a Jesuit priest, and before his return to England and eventual martyrdom, he engaged largely in educational activities, teaching the liberal arts, especially philosophy and rhetoric at a Jesuit school, as well as giving displays of oratory and writing and producing plays. To a decisive extent, Campion embodied the qualities that Newman would readily identify, three centuries later, with his "idea of a university." And they both embody, I believe, the Catholic intellectual vocation, consisting as it does of certain distinctive attributes, notably, a devotion to truth, the synthesis of faith and reason, an attitude of spiritual sacrifice and fidelity, a zeal for souls, and a certain daring in challenging the status quo.

These qualities have registered an impact on our religious and educational culture, not least in the names of Campion and Newman being invoked by various institutions (tertiary colleges, university clubs and residential halls, and secondary schools). I am myself associated with such an institution in Sydney, a university-level Catholic Liberal Arts college called Campion College Australia. Our reason for adopting the name of Campion flowed from his universal status as a scholar, martyr and saint, but also from his local links with Australia. He has long served as the patron saint of lay Catholic adult education in Australia, beginning in the 1930s when the Campion Society was born, and occurring again in the 1970s when the Campion Fellowship arose—the name of that Fellowship being harvested, several years later, by this very body in the United States, the Fellowship of Catholic Scholars.

This spirit of intellectual vocation, and the qualities it embodies, are strikingly evident in both Campion and Newman. In his biography of Campion, Evelyn Waugh describes the process by which the Elizabethan scholar and saint came to realize what God was asking of him, in his fidelity to the truth, and to God:

> Only by slow stages was it revealed to Campion how complete was the sacrifice required of him. He had powerful friends and a brilliant reputation. Surely with these it must still be possible to make a career in the world, without doing violence to his religion? Surely it was not expected of him to give up all?[12]

In the case of Newman, too, the process of realization was slow and yet remorseless. He was acutely conscious of the sacrifices, both personal and social, he made in becoming a Catholic; and he lamented the loss of old associations and the displacement of memories.[13] His last sermon as an Anglican was called "The Parting of Friends."[14] He felt no personal consolations or rewards in the years following his conversion to Catholicism; having to endure, on the one hand, grievous misunderstanding, and, on the other hand, repeated neglect of his talents and his potential value to the Church.[15] In this, no doubt, he underwent a continuing torment, as was experienced in the following century by another priest-convert from Anglicanism, Ronald Knox, who, in the words of a recent reviewer, suffered "a mild martyrdom."[16] Even the pangs of intellectual confession were sharply felt: in writing the *Apologia pro Vita Sua* (1864), Newman reported being "constantly in tears, and constantly crying out with distress."[17]

Both Campion and Newman understood that the Catholic intellectual vocation involved suffering—suffering for the truth, and suffering for souls. One mark of this was the battle for truth in the various controversies in which Campion and Newman engaged. Campion showed his willingness and his skill in the work of apologetics he produced, *Ten Reasons,* and in his *Brag*, the short but crucial manifesto he wrote of his purpose in returning to England; as well as, following his capture, in the verbal defense he offered, during his trial, of the Catholic mission which he and others had undertaken in England.

Newman, for his part, revealed at an early date his taste as well as his talent for controversy. As his biographer, Ian Ker, has observed, Newman had a strongly logical mind and great powers of irony and sarcasm, which were especially effective in his satirical writings.[18]

The involvement of Campion and Newman in controversy—in the great debates of their respective times—it is of instructive interest in relation to their contrasting personalities. Campion was a strikingly attractive figure. At Oxford he gained a loyal following among students; they flocked to his lectures and even imitated his mannerisms and dress style. He was a man of gentle courtesy but he was not reserved, delighting in oratory and the theatre. His biographer, Evelyn Waugh, describes him as "magnetic and inspiring."[19] Across the centuries, he comes to us as a man of unmistakable flair.

Newman appears as a different personality, reserved, even shy; lonely and highly sensitive, though also robust in the face of adversity; and, living as he did so much longer than Campion, he was much affected by the enfeeblement of age.

I have emphasized, in exploring the witness that Campion and Newman gave to the Catholic intellectual vocation, their readiness to suffer for the truth. But a further dimension of their vocation was their willingness to suffer for souls. These are organically linked, in imitation of Christ's own statement, that "I am the Way, the Truth and the Life" (John 14:6); but they are also treated in *The Idea of a University*, where Newman argues that, while the direct end of a university is knowledge, the indirect effects of a university are religious.[20]

In Campion's case, there is his heroic virtue as a priest, at first during his six years at Prague, where he not only served an academic role, but was also a preacher and confessor and provider of succor to those in prison and in hospital; and then on his return to England where he faced the hazards of being a hunted priest as he ministered to his persecuted flock. One incident in particular, I think, epitomizes his pastoral ardor, and that is, his forgiveness of the man, George Eliot, who betrayed him to the authorities. (One might discern here the shades of Pope John Paul II, forgiving Mehmet Ali Agca in his Rome prison cell, following the assassination attempt by the latter in 1981.) George Eliot visited Campion in his prison cell and confessed that, after his Judas-like act, he feared for his life. Campion urged him to seek God's mercy and do penance for the sake of his salvation. He then offered to provide for Eliot's safety by recommending him to a Catholic duke in Germany. This overture did not have the desired effect. Eliot returned to spying for the Protestant authorities. But it did produce another benefit. Campion's gaoler was present at his meeting with Eliot and was so swayed by Campion's greatness of heart that he became a Catholic.

Newman, too, exhibited a readiness to suffer for souls. His conversion to Catholicism did not loosen his bonds of sympathy with his Anglican friends. He recalled with feeling the long years where they worshipped side-by-side, but acknowledged that his very outspokenness was due to his conviction that "the Catholic Church is the one ark of salvation,"[21] and due also to the love that he harbored for their souls. As a priest, he had a deep pastoral sense, which his fame and his final elevation to be a cardinal did not impair. Those whom God "singularly and specially loves, He pursued with His blows, sometimes on one and the same wound, till perhaps they are tempted to cry out for mercy."[22] Newman, indeed, thought that the very act of belief was not only intellectual but also moral. It depends on "a right state of heart" and "is perfected, not by intellectual cultivation, but by obedience." In short, Newman said, "We *believe*, because we *love.*"[23]

An important factor in the zeal for souls exhibited by both Campion and Newman, I believe, was their exposure to popular Catholic culture and ordinary Catholic people. As Campion wrestled at Oxford with his mind and conscience over his religious allegiance, it proved significant that he moved to Ireland. There he lived in the family home of a friend, and, Evelyn Waugh records, "for the first and last time in his life, he tasted the happiness of a normal, cultured household."[24] He experienced the tribal life of the Irish people, and the dependable routines and rhythms of a deeply Catholic culture.

Newman was also exposed to this Irish culture, during the seven years of his effort to establish the Catholic University in Dublin. He felt an enduring gratitude to the Irish people for the kindness they had shown him over the years from his first visit in 1851. But at an earlier stage, both before and after his conversion, he had visited Italy and Sicily. He was profoundly impressed by the quality of popular faith; "*everywhere* [he found] a simple certainty in believing which to a Protestant or Anglican is quite astonishing."[25] Newman also understood the nature of popular faith which, while it was often intermingled with pagan traditions and included superstitions requiring purification, was nonetheless far preferable to scepticism. "[He] who believes a little, but encompasses that little with the inventions of men, is undeniably in a better condition than he who blots out from his mind both the human inventions, and that portion of truth which was concealed in them."[26]

The culture of popular belief and practice is central to the contributions of Campion and Newman to the cause of Catholic higher education. Both were engaged in disputes that seemed ecclesiastical and political, and appeared to be essentially conflicts between Catholicism and Protestantism. They were, however, actually far more profound, involving conflicts that were spiritual, and even apocalyptic. For both men recognized that new forces were menacing the Christian faith and, by extension, its institutions such as the Catholic university. Like Thomas More before him, Campion saw the threat posed by the power of the state when it was enlisted in a way that damaged the unity of the Church, and allowed political and earthly allegiance to become synonymous with religious and transcendental faithfulness.

Newman, on the other hand, was particularly alive to the looming danger of secularism—a threat to the fundamental viability of religious belief in Western society which was not only becoming irreligious but anti-Christian.

As Christopher Dawson pointed out, "Newman was the first

Christian thinker in the English-speaking world who fully realized the nature of modern secularism and the enormous change which was already in the process of development, although a century had still to pass before it was to produce its full harvest of destruction."[27]

In a remarkable sermon which Newman preached in 1873 entitled "The Infidelity of the Future," he foresaw the magnitude of the threat posed by a militant secularism. "Christianity," he said, "has never yet had experience of a world simply irreligious," and "the trials which lie before us are such as would appall and make dizzy even such courageous hearts as St. Athansius, St. Gregory I, or St. Gregory VII. And they would confess that, dark as the prospect of their own day was to them severally, ours has a darkness different in kind from any that has been before it."[28] It was no longer possible to depend on the orthodox faith of Protestants, while Catholics in England were likely to be seen as the "enemies" of "civil liberty" and "national progress," and to face discrimination, particularly since they were too prominent to be ignored and yet too weak to defend themselves.[29]

Both Campion and Newman possessed a prophetic sense that remains sharply relevant to our own times, and to the future of a Catholic university in our society. Frank Sheed said that Campion was "the first modern man in English history...He was of 20th century cast."[30] Campion was sensitive to the problem of the state in relation to the Church, especially when it came to the enforcement of false religion.

No doubt the people of the 16th century were feeling their way on the precise relationship of religious and political institutions, especially when they fell into conflict over the primacy of a citizen's loyalty. But it is perhaps arguable that Campion saw with special clarity the extent to which the State could subject the prerogatives of God to the power of Caesar, and produce the beginnings of a politicized Church—and a desacralized state—with which we are much more familiar today.

Newman, too, grappled with the issue of a state Church, but I think he extended his gaze beyond that ecclesiastical and political level to the more pervasive problems of culture and faith itself.

A politicized Church brings the power of the state into the very bosom of the Church, so that the state determines and dictates rather than simply supporting religious faith; this is a reversal of right order which leads to a fatal confusion of sacred and secular loyalties. There are abundant examples of this confusion in present-day Western society, particularly in the sphere of law, whether it is of the legislature or of the courts; but perhaps the most striking instance of a politicized Church is present-day Islam, which compounds religion and politics in a social order that is also elevated—indeed, one might say, consecrated—by the impulses of nationalism.

The lack of distinction in Islam between Church and state, between God and Caesar—and, indeed, between faith and reason—constitutes, of course, a direct and often violent confrontation with the complacent yet tenacious secularism of the contemporary West. I think the resurgence of Islam in the 21st century has given new relevance, and a new urgency, to the events and consequences of the 16th century English Reformation. Indeed, if Islam poses the great threat to Christianity in the 21st century, as Communism did in the 20th century, we can appreciate even more sharply the combined importance for our time of the prophetic insights of Edmund Campion and John Henry Newman. Campion may, indeed, be seen as a precursor of Newman, for, if the state can determine religion, it can also determine irreligion. It can impose apostasy. A politicized Church, in which the temporal displaces the transcendental, paves the way for a secularist culture, in which temporal loyalties are elevated to the level of the timeless, and totalitarian ideology becomes a substitute for transcendental faith.

These principles are of direct relevance to the university as an institution, and, specifically, to the Catholic university; for the university cannot maintain its integrity, and its essential mission, as an educational institution, if it is at first politicized and then secularized.

If I may quote Christopher Dawson once again: in his 1961 book, *The Crisis of Western Education*, Dawson noted—I think, with great prescience—that, in a secularist culture, the Catholic Church must not only deal with Catholic colleges and universities. It must attend to secular institutions of learning as well.[31] So, in exploring the idea of a *Catholic* university in the 21st century, we must also address, I believe, the idea of a *university*.

I have described Campion and Newman, in the sub-title of this paper, as the Peter and Paul of Catholic higher education. I hope that this is not too provocative a proposal; and, if it is, I hope you will pardon it as a piece of poetic license, attributing it to the difficulty which we Australians face in walking upside down at the bottom of the world! However, in pondering the importance of Campion and Newman, both for their own time and for ours, I have been struck by certain parallels with the lives and contributions of St. Peter and St. Paul.

In their sense of *intellectual* vocation, Campion and Newman may be seen to resemble St. Paul. This is seen in their facility with ideas and with language, in their deep convictions founded in faith as well as reason, and in their devotion to learning. St. Paul was a convert, as were both Campion and Newman; and, just as St. Paul provided a theological foundation and an intellectual architecture for the Christian faith, so Campion and Newman supplied the intellectual underpinning for the Christian university.

In certain other ways, Campion and Newman again both resemble St. Paul: in their preaching and power of oratory, and in their daring, a brave eagerness to take on the prevailing intellectual order and challenge it with the Truth of Christ To this might be added Campion's personal prowess, a *physical* daring, an undeniable verve, as also manifested by St. Paul in his perilous journeys, and by St. Edmund Campion in his period of constantly evading the English authorities, until, like St. Paul, he was finally captured and martyred.

Newman, too, displays Pauline qualities. For one thing, Newman and St. Paul were great letter writers. For another, they both sought to adapt the Church to new conditions, Newman's grasp of secularism helping to prepare the Church for a different culture, mirroring St. Paul's role in developing the Church beyond its cradle in Judaism in order to meet the different circumstances of a Gentile world.

Newman had a special respect for St. Paul because of his humanity, "his intimate sympathy and compassionateness for the whole world, not only in its strength, but in its weakness; in the lively regard with which he views everything that comes before him, taken in the concrete."[32]

Campion and Newman resemble St. Peter in the unmistakable qualities of leadership which each displayed. They embodied and projected a vision of learning, of the intellectual apostolate, and of the university, that bears respectful comparison with the broader leadership in the Church exercised by St. Peter. They also showed a capacity for *organizational* development, one of the qualities of a leader, as revealed in their respective desire to found universities in Ireland, and in Newman's case, in his establishment of the Oratory in Birmingham as an institutional center of Christian humanism.

An incidental link of St. Edmund Campion with St. Peter, which I find intriguing, is that the day on which Campion resigned from Oxford (in 1569), and embarked upon the path that finally led to his martyrdom, was the feast of St. Peter in Chains; this was surely a symbolic prefigurement for Campion himself. And, after his return to England in 1580, Campion chose the feast day of St. Peter and St. Paul, June 29, to speak on the papacy (under the title *"Tu es Petrus"*) before a large audience in London.

It would, I believe, be appropriate that, if John Henry Newman is finally raised to the altars of Catholic sainthood, he should share the feast day of St. Edmund Campion, December 1st—in a graceful echo of the combined feast day of St. Peter and St. Paul (on June 29).

Karl G. Schmude is an Australian who has combined university librarianship with free-lance writing and speaking, both in his homeland and internationally. After serving as director of libraries at a rural university in Australia, he recently played a leading part in the creation of a Catholic liberal arts institution, Campion College Australia, which opened in Sydney in 2006. He is also executive director of the Campion Foundation. He has enjoyed a long association with the Fellowship of Catholic Scholars, having attended its first meeting in 1977.

Endnotes

[1]Richard Simpson, *Edmund Campion: A Biography* (London: John Hodges, 1896), p.20.

[2]C.S. Dessain, *John Henry Newman* (London: Nelson, 1966), p.6. Cf., the comment of Christopher Dawson, *The Spirit of the Oxford Movement* (London: Sheed & Ward, 1933), p.87: "[Newman] saw that the anti-modern character of Oxford, its unutilitarian beauty, fitted it to be the representative of religious ideals and spiritual values in an age of secularism and material progress."

[3]Ian Ker, *John Henry Newman: A Biography* (Oxford: Oxford University Press, 1988), p.493.

[4]Simpson, *Edmund Campion*, p.21; and *The Letters and Diaries of John Henry Newman*, Ed., Charles Stephen Dessain et al. (Oxford: Clarendon, 1961-77), Vol.XXI, p.303.

[5]John Henry Newman, *Fifteen Sermons Preached Before the University of Oxford* (London: Longmans, Green & Co, 1900), Sermons X and XI, pp.176-221.

[6]*Letters and Diaries*, Vol.XXI, p.327; and John Henry Newman, *The Idea of a University*, ed. I.T. Ker (Oxford: Clarendon, 1976), p.392.

[7]Ker, *John Henry Newman*, pp.382-3.

[8]Simpson, *Edmund Campion*, p.34.

[9]C.C. Martindale SJ, *Blessed Edmund Campion* (London: Catholic Truth Society, 1964), p.3.

[10]Simpson, *Edmund Campion*, p.33.

[11]*Ibid*, pp.36-7.

[12]Evelyn Waugh, *Edmund Campion* (London: Longmans, Green & Co, 1935), p.33.

[13]Ker, *John Henry Newman*, p.293.

[14]John Henry Newman, *Sermons Bearing on Subjects of the Day* (London: Rivington, 1844), pp. 447-64.

[15]Ker, *John Henry Newman*, pp.520, 561.

[16]Isabel Quigly, "Mild and Bitter," *Times Literary Supplement* (29 March 2002), p.36.

[17]*Letters and Diaries*, Vol.XXI, p.107.

[18]Ker, *John Henry Newman*, pp.157, 168.

[19]Waugh, *Edmund Campion*, p.62.

[20]Ker, *John Henry Newman*, p.381.

[21]John Henry Newman, *Certain Difficulties felt by Anglicans in Catholic Teaching* (London: Longmans, Green & Co, 1918), Vol.1, p.4.

[22]Ker, *John Henry Newman*, pp.709-10.

[23]John Henry Newman, *Fifteen Sermons Preached before the University of Oxford* (London: Longmans,, Green & Co, 1900), pp.234,236,250.

[24]Waugh, *Edmund Campion*, p.34.

[25]Letters and Diaries, Vol.XII, p.24.

[26]John Henry Newman, *The Arians of the Fourth Century* (London: Longmans, Green & Co, 1895), p.85.

[27]Christopher Dawson, "Newman and the Sword of the Spirit," *The Sword of the Spirit* (August 1945), p.1.

[28]John Henry Newman, *Catholic Sermons of Cardinal Newman* (London: Burns & Oates, 1957), pp.121, 123.

[29]Ker, *John Henry Newman*, p.676.

[30]F.J. Sheed, *Sidelights on the Catholic Revival* (London: Catholic Book Club, 1940), p.19.

[31]Christopher Dawson, *The Crisis of Western Education* (London: Sheed & Ward, 1961), p.112.

[32]Ker, *John Henry Newman*, p.484

The State of the Question: Models for Catholic Universities

Measuring Catholic Claims

Melanie M. Morey and John J. Piderit, S.J.

Introduction

A STANDARD MANTRA in management circles, both outside and inside higher education, is this: If you don't measure it, you don't manage it. In its general form, the claim is actually a fairly weak one, since it states that an administrator cannot effectively manage an issue without getting data about how it is progressing, regressing, morphing, or remaining the same. In most cases, administrators have some data, even if the data does not change much from year to year. But if that data does not change much from year to year, it is safe to conclude that the administrator is not managing the area in any active sense. The manager might have some ideas about how to improve services or cut costs in the particular area and may discuss these proposals with other administrators and then decide to implement one or two programs. But without some fairly regularly updated data to review, there is no feedback mechanism which indicates the impact of the program. The administrator in that case is making changes from time to time, but those changes are not necessarily influenced by any data regularly received and reviewed.

Management theory warns managers that they need regularly updated data to adequately supervise an area. The more important the area, the more regular, accurate, and pertinent the feedback data should be. This paper accepts this administrative meta-rule as a helpful one for university and college administrators. In fact, in many areas of Catholic and non-sectarian university life, administrators adhere to this rule. Most private colleges and universities depend predominantly on tuition revenues to run their institutions. Not surprisingly, presidents and boards of trustees regularly review data on the application funnel: the number of inquiries, the number of applications, the geographical dispersal of applications, the number of students who register for classes in the fall, the summer melt, the academic profile of both applicants and registrants, etc. Academics themselves regularly measure student progress in order to gauge the extent to which students acquire knowledge, and they also ask students to evaluate courses which they have taken. Administrators and staff keep detailed records on the number of students in the residence halls, the number using various meal plans, the number of rule infractions by students, etc. All these examples are part and parcel of general operating procedures at most colleges and universities. Our focus in this essay is on one area of Catholic collegiate management that seldom gets measured and probably would benefit it if did—the particularly Catholic components of institutional mission.

Foundations

How "Catholic" Catholic institutions really are in the United States has been the subject of much discussion and debate over the last decade or so. Unfortunately, when it comes to understanding exactly what it means or should mean for an institution to call itself Catholic, the category of Catholic identity proves not to be all that helpful. In analyzing the data from a national study of Catholic higher education,[1] it became clear to us that culture, and particularly organizational culture, is a more robust category for framing the discussion. Culture is the subject of a significant body of research and literature that can illuminate the discussion. This category is particularly useful for understanding the nature of institutional Catholic character and mission. It also is a useful construct for exploring what effective institutions are in terms of accomplishing their stated "Catholic" goals. Culture results from the interaction of *actions* and *inheritance*. *Actions* are the present choices people within a culture make about activities, what to do and how to behave. *Inheritance* is the operative context for actions that resulted from previous choices made.

Generally speaking, culture is a pattern of activity (how things are done around here) that an identifiable group regularly encounters. Culture is fluid, not static and it adapts and changes. Fundamental aspects within cultures determine whether they progress or wither over time. This is true for cultures be they corporate cultures, entertainment cultures, professional cultures, or religious cultures. In terms of Catholic colleges and universities, when we examine the array of ways they have to explore, understand, integrate, and support faith, we are studying the Catholic culture at the university.

Cultures are comprised of content, symbols and actors. Cultural content includes beliefs, values, norms, and shared assumptions that guide how people act. Cultural symbols are the glue that makes it possible for cultures to adhere. Rituals, art, architecture, images, sagas, other narratives and stories and heroic exemplars are all cultural symbols. Finally, all cultures have actors, the men and women who bring the culture to life. Some cultural actors are cultural citizens who sustain culture by their own regular participation in symbolic events and who share the content of culture with the people with whom they are in contact. At Catholic colleges and universities that includes students, administrators, faculty, staff, alumni, donors, etc.

Cultural actions also include cultural catalysts who provide cultural leadership and take initiatives to make catalyzing adjustments in the culture in response to demands of the times. In order to remain both vibrant and viable, culture needs to be sustained through the actions of its cultural citizens and revitalized through the initiatives of cultural catalysts.

Distinguishability and Inheritability

In order to conduct a helpful examination of Catholic universities, it is also important to understand that in order to remain vital and viable, every culture must be both distinguishable and inheritable.

In order to be distinguishable, the impact of content, symbols, and actors in a culture has to be such that anyone looking at it can see how it is clearly different from the cultures of other organizations involved in similar activities. Furthermore, that distinguishability has to be real and apparent in the primary activities of the organization.

In terms of colleges and universities, their most central activity is the academic enterprise, and in Catholic colleges and universities, the Catholic character of the enterprise should be distinguishable in this setting.

A second necessary quality of a healthy culture is that it can and likely will be effectively passed on to the next generation of students. That is, the program at the Catholic college has to be such that it is inheritable. Inheritability means the institution has good reason to believe that the academic and social programs under the direction of the college or university have sufficiently broad appeal that, despite changes in society, the next generation of students will continue to be attracted to the institution. In any given year, the number of applications may fall because of competitive moves by other institutions. But an inheritable culture has sufficient depth that it can rebound, though perhaps with some difficulty.

Inheritability embraces a number of more specific conditions. It certainly implies financial stability. The institution must have a program that attracts enough students so that the university can pay all its bills and also offer the type of education it says it offers. But it also means that the college must attract students who have an interest in the Catholic identity. Would it be possible in the United States to have a Catholic institution in which practically none of the faculty or students was a practicing Catholic? We don't think so. This does not mean that everyone has to be Catholic, but if a Catholic institution can't attract a substantial group of Catholic students and faculty to its institution, then the Catholic culture at the institution will not be inheritable.

In order to stay viable, cultures must also be adept at making adjustments over time. Some adaptations will respond to external forces such as changes in competing cultures. Others will be prompted by internal forces. Regardless of what precipitates the adaptations, the end result will be the same—a difference in cultural content and symbols and in the behavior of cultural actors. A culture that lacks flexibility in the face of internal and external pressure to change will cease to be inheritable.

A Few Characteristics of Catholic Higher Education

Catholic colleges and universities have an interest in promoting Catholic belief, understanding, and practice that distinguishes them from their non-Catholic counterparts. This interest is an integral part of the mission of any Catholic college or university that is reflected in its core academic activity. So, at the very least, a Catholic university has some informed and trained faculty members knowledgeable about the Catholic faith who teach courses which have significant bearing on the Catholic faith. Usually, a Catholic college or university has at least a religious studies department or, better, a theology department, which offers courses in which one can explore the academic underpinnings of the Catholic faith. What other courses in the institution touch upon the Catholic faith varies with the size and mission of the institution. Later in this paper, we will explore a broader array of possible academic offerings which touch upon Catholic faith and the Catholic Church.

Before proceeding too far in this presentation, it is important to emphasize that the Catholic faith does not exist independent of the Catholic Church. A person comes to believe and accept the Catholic faith through baptism into the Catholic Church. A person is nurtured in the faith within the Catholic Church, most importantly within the local parish community. By participating in and receiving the Eucharist and other sacraments in a parish, a Catholic draws strength to serve others from a community which together tries to live the faith as conscientiously as possible. Even when all the local parish communities are joined together under the Vicar of Christ in Rome, this is only a part of the Church. The Catholic Church also includes those who participate in the heavenly banquet as well as those in purgatory who are being purified so that they can one day participate in the heavenly banquet.

The Catholic faith simply does not exist apart from the Catholic Church, which hands on the faith, nourishes it, and formulates it in ways more or less appropriate for modern society. Courses in Catholic theology explore how the Catholic Church understands itself in relation to the revelation contained in the Bible as interpreted in the Catholic tradition. The witness of the Bible is that God's revelation reaches its fulfillment in Jesus Christ. Theology explores the epitome of this fulfillment and then seeks greater understanding by integrating it with its historical development and in relation to the modern world.

Given this self-understanding of the Church, a Catholic university does not restrict itself solely to sharing and developing knowledge about how the Church understands itself. Through campus ministry, all Catholic colleges and universities also offer students, faculty, and staff opportunities to practice the faith and also encourage those who are Catholic to intensify their commitment to their Catholic faith.

One can, therefore, distinguish three important religious goals of any Catholic university. The first goal of a Catholic institution of higher education is to inform students (and perhaps faculty and staff as well, but certainly students) about how the Catholic Church understands itself. The second goal is to offer students opportunities to practice the Catholic faith. Because students are young and changing, the third goal pertains to their commitment to the Catholic faith. A Catholic college or university encourages students to deepen their commitment to the Catholic faith during their years of study at the college or university.

Most Catholic institutions of higher education also have two additional goals they share with many of their non-Catholic counterparts. First, they seek to graduate students who will be leaders or influential people in society. And second, they hope the educational experience their students receive during these formative years will so shape their way of thinking and acting that the effects will last a lifetime.

Curious Discrepancies

In *Catholic Higher Education: A Culture in Crisis*, we note an academic pattern at most institutions of higher education and then highlight a rather startling academic lacuna in one particular area proper to Catholic institutions of higher education.[2] Sometime prior to the beginning of classes in the fall, most freshmen, depending on their college and intended major, take a battery of placement tests. They take a math placement test to determine what type of introductory math course will be most appropriate for them. Similarly, they take a modern language placement exam to determine how proficient they have become in the modern language they studied in high school. Many institutions require a writing sample to determine which entering freshmen require more instruction and practice in writing essays. There would probably be more such exploratory exams were it not the case that freshmen take many "placement exams."[3] The scores of these exams are submitted to the college or university and are part of the student's profile. Thus, in particular subjects such as history, science, and literature, many colleges and universities have a good deal of information about the academic achievement level of their students.

We are familiar with no Catholic college or university that offers or requires a "Catholic knowledge" placement exam for entering undergraduates. Admittedly, the SAT and ACT do not offer such a test. However, it would not be difficult for a theology department at a Catholic university, either by itself or working jointly with several other Catholic institutions, to devise such an exam. It is truly curious that Catholic colleges and universities have so far not considered it important to determine the range of "Catholic knowledge" among entering students. Anecdotal information from theology faculty suggests that only a few entering students are knowledgeable about the Catholic faith, while most are woefully uninformed.

Faculty members in disciplines other than theology require entering students to take placement exams because when the knowledge base of the students is extremely uneven, teaching is difficult, and outcomes are often unsatisfying. In these circumstances, faculty demand, and get, greater homogeneity in classes with respect to knowledge. The placement exams are used to group the students according to their knowledge or skill in handling the material.

Theology departments are not offering Catholic knowledge placement exams. One possible reason may be that, unlike their colleagues in other departments, theology and religious studies faculty are not pressing for them. It may be that the fraction of students with little knowledge of the Catholic faith represents that vast majority of students in introductory theology classes and teachers can conveniently teach to their level. That approach allows the better informed students to get an "easy A" in a not-so-demanding course ("easy" because the well informed students already know most of the material being covered).

Whatever may be the views of the theology faculty, the lack of a placement exam communicates information to students, parents, and Catholic high schools whose graduates attend Catholic colleges or universities. The absence of a placement exam in Catholic knowledge signals that it really does not matter how much Catholic knowledge the students get during their high school years. Even if they learned practically nothing, the faculty at the Catholic university will accept the students and make appropriate adjustments in the introductory theology courses at the Catholic college or university.

The potential impact of a Catholic knowledge placement exam on Catholic high schools should not be underestimated. Should a Catholic college or university institute such an exam, Catholic high schools would take notice. If, for example, the local Catholic high school over the past three years sent ten students to a particular Catholic college or university and none of the high school graduates did well on the Catholic knowledge placement exam, both parents and administrators would demand better results.

Some might object that requiring entering students to take such an exam would disadvantage the non-Catholic students. That may be partially true, but it may not be generally true for most non-Catholic students. Some of these students could well have fairly good knowledge of Catholic teachings. Furthermore, many students belonging to various Protestant denominations may have far more extensive knowledge of the Bible than their Catholic counterparts, and this type of knowledge would presumably constitute a significant portion of any Catholic knowledge placement exam.

If a Catholic college or university asked or required students to take a Catholic knowledge placement exam, those students taking the exam and doing well on it could be offered the opportunity to take a theology course which explores more deeply the material to be covered in the general introductory course. Alternatively, students scoring well on the Catholic knowledge placement exam might take their introductory course from a popular member of the theology department who is well-respected by the students.

Expanding the Set of Recommended Catholic Courses

The most important discipline at a Catholic university should be theology and, indeed, most Catholic universities require students to take one or two courses in theology or religious studies. Acknowledging the important distinction between theology and religious studies, it is also important to note the wide variety of content in introductory courses in theology. Much of the content appears to depend on the interests of the faculty member who teaches the course. Despite the course title, the first or second course in theology required at a Catholic university may in fact offer very little systematic material on Catholic teachings. Furthermore, as R. R. Reno has pointed out, in many cases the faculty members teaching theology courses at the undergraduate or graduate level may not have a sufficient grounding themselves in what he calls standard theology.[4]

Related to the possibility of a Catholic knowledge placement exam is the issue of foundational knowledge needed in various academic disciplines which interest undergraduate students.[5] In order to understand various classical authors (those taught in the canon) in English literature, students need more than a passing familiarity with important stories in the Old and New Testament. For this reason, it can make good sense to offer or require students in English literature to take a course entitled "The Bible as Literature."[6] Such a course would treat the Bible as literature and examine those passages or parts to which English authors make frequent allusion. This literary approach, of course, would be distinct from the approach taken in a theology course on the Bible, which would focus perhaps on how the Bible is understood as the revealed word of God, how it came to be written, and how it forms the basis for all doctrines of the Catholic Church.

At a Catholic college or university it makes sense to offer a variety of such discipline-focused courses relating to the Catholic or generally Christian faith. Catholic universities typically emphasize the importance of Catholic social teaching. This teaching has important implications for political science, sociology, economics, and business. Having a course entitled "Biblical Foundations of Christian Justice" would be a helpful one for students in one of the social sciences. They could take this course in their junior or senior year, by which time they would already be familiar with the contours of their discipline. Similarly, a well structured course aimed at students in science or engineering could accomplish two goals. First, in a more Catholic philosophical and theological vein, it could delimit the contours of which issues science says it can handle and which ones it says it cannot treat, by reason of the methods it uses. Second, such a course would take seriously the many purported violations of the physical laws of the universe depicted in the Bible and it would offer a perspective which allows students to appreciate the outstanding contributions of science at the same time that it highlights the valuable knowledge which a Christian believer can garner from Scripture. Invoking philosophical and theological distinctions makes it possible to allay student concerns that there are fundamental conflicts which require them to choose one path of knowledge over the other.

Another valuable academic course for many Catholic undergraduates is a history of Catholicism. Some Catholic colleges and universities have a single survey course which would be suitable as an introductory course, but most have components of it in various courses focusing on a particular era or theme. Among history faculty, such survey courses are no longer popular. Because they cover such a broad expanse and because historians now specialize with respect to historical periods as well as themes within a particular historical period, many historians do not consider themselves sufficiently well informed to offer survey course of the Church that covers its two thousand years.

Despite the reluctance of historians to offer this type of course, history is now an important axis for Catholics to come to a deeper understanding of their faith and the Church. One of the fundamental developments which occurred in the 19th and 20th centuries is the realization that human beings and institutions have developed gradually over time. Although the essential structure of the Catholic Church is the same today as in the early centuries of its existence, the actual structures have taken very different shape over the centuries. It would be helpful for Catholic graduates of Catholic colleges and universities to be familiar with these developments. For this reason, it would be good for a percentage of the baccalaureate class to have taken a course on the history of the Catholic Church. We are not suggesting a required course in the history of Catholicism, but rather one which is generally recommended to students. We will return to the issue of incentives a little later.

Fifty years ago, philosophy constituted the bulk of the required courses at Catholic colleges and universities. The approximately eight courses students were required to take were the rough equivalent of a major or minor in philosophy today.[7] The courses included logic, epistemology, rational psychology, cosmology, metaphysics, the history of philosophy, natural theology, and ethics. These subjects offered students a way to critically evaluate much of what they learned in college or university and much of what they would encounter later in life. While some smaller Catholic colleges still offer some of these subjects, many are no longer offered in philosophy departments at many Catholic colleges and universities.

Some of the traditional subject matter in philosophy is no

longer considered of interest even to philosophers. The traditional material that is still taught is sometimes found in other academic departments. In the instances where this material is still treated in the philosophy department, it is bundled together in different topic groupings within courses that have very different names. Alternatively, material previously covered in philosophy courses has migrated to other academic disciplines. Ethics, for example, used to be taught only in philosophy and frequently there were two courses: theoretical ethics and applied ethics. General ethics and its principles are still taught in many philosophy departments, but most of the applied ethics courses have moved to departments such as business, nursing, accounting, law, and medicine.

One reason for the migration of philosophical material to other academic departments is that academic departments have become more independent and, in some cases, even imperious in their demands. Faculty in particular academic departments designate the number of required courses plus the number of electives. At many colleges, students effectively spend four complete semesters taking courses in their primary or secondary major. Majors count much more today than they did fifty years ago, in part because students must take the equivalent of a full year of courses in their major. This means that time for other electives is quite limited. It would be helpful, therefore, for interested students to have the opportunity in two or three courses to learn some of the helpful approaches once covered in philosophy but now applied to an area of knowledge that encompasses their specific academic major. Many Catholic colleges and universities still require students to take one or two courses in philosophy. It would be helpful if these institutions also offered a single course that introduced students to a Catholic philosophical approach useful within particular disciplines. As we argued above for biblical courses oriented to groups of academic disciplines, a similar approach would be helpful for philosophy. Thus, there might be courses entitled "Catholic Philosophy for Majors in the Social Sciences," "The Catholic Approach to Law and Government," "The Catholic Philosophy of Beauty," or "Catholic Philosophical Issues in the Natural Sciences." Many Catholic institutions already have a course which focuses on Catholic social teachings. The additional courses we propose here would not focus primarily on ethics, since there are other courses in most colleges or universities which address those issues. Rather, the courses would start from a Catholic worldview and show what the boundaries and benefits are of the individual disciplines.

More Carrots than Sticks

Undergraduate students at most colleges and universities are allowed to exercise considerable choice in the courses they select. Even in the courses they take to fulfill area requirements or requirements for their majors, they have considerable latitude. As indicated above, many students have sufficient leeway in their undergraduate schedule that they can fulfill the requirements for a primary as well as a secondary major. Given this flexibility, it is possible for a Catholic college or university to use the attraction principle to take courses which administration deems particularly useful in understanding and appreciating the Catholic world view.

It is possible for the dean of one or more colleges to initiate a program that encourages students to take six courses with high Catholic content, some of which are related to the student's primary major. The dean might say that anyone who fulfills the requirements will be given the designation "Catholic Scholar," and this title would appear on the scholar's diploma at graduation. For many students with perhaps only an inchoate interest in Catholic teaching and practices, this incentive will be sufficient to get them to take some courses they might otherwise have overlooked.[8]

A Catholic Scholars program is another way to get students engaged in discussion with other students about Catholic issues. Students in the Catholic Scholars program could be invited to participate in a four-day, start-of-the-semester seminar. The seminar might consist of faculty speaking on an announced theme. In addition, faculty teaching courses in the program as well as other faculty would attend the seminar to listen to students as some students presented their own research papers on some aspect of the same Catholic theme. This would prepare students to be alert to Catholic themes during their junior and senior years at college.[9]

If an even greater incentive were needed to attract a larger number of students, those who are close to receiving the designation "Catholic Scholar" would be allowed to participate in a special two-week course in Rome over a Christmas break. The course would be led by someone knowledgeable about Christian art, architecture, and history. All students participating would already have some background in Catholic knowledge and they would also have displayed a commitment to learning more about their Catholic faith, both in terms of how it developed and how it should be preached, practiced, and prayed in modern society. A Rome seminar with this orientation would be a wonderful cap-stone experience for the students. Most of the attraction would be visiting the sites in Rome, much would emanate from the teachers, but much of the fun and learning for students would consist in being with a group of students who take their Catholic faith seriously.

Were a Catholic college or university to develop a fairly broad based type of Catholic Scholars program, it could also provide a guide for the type of expertise required among the faculty and what percentage of them should be practicing Catholic. As we argue in our book, *Ex Corde Ecclesiae* is correct to focus on the proportion of Catholic faculty members at a Catholic institution. In the book we argue that the percentage of informed, committed Catholics among the faculty must be large enough to have an impact on the students targeted by the university.[10] The percentage must also be large enough so that they enjoy influence and respect in Catholic matters among the other faculty. In matters pertaining to Catholic mission, there have to be sufficient faculty of sufficient influence and stature that other faculty members defer to them with respect to Catholic academic issues.

Using a Catholic Scholars program as a lever enables one to calculate more carefully the number of informed, committed and practicing Catholics among the faculty needed to make an impact on the targeted group of students. At a minimum, one needs a sufficient number of Catholic faculty members to teach the various Catholic philosophy courses as well as a course in each discipline which emphasizes Catholic themes related to the discipline. The Catholic Scholars program described here is designed to have at least two "Catholic courses" in a student's major. Therefore, there would have to be a sufficiently broad distribution of informed, committed faculty across various academic departments in order for students aspiring to be Catholic Scholars to be able to take their "Catholic courses" in a timely manner.[11]

Since the goal is to help these students understand, practice, and deepen their faith, they will benefit most by an experienced person who is not only knowledgeable about the faith but who is also committed to it and practices it. For this reason, all these courses should be taught by practicing Catholics.

We have described at some length what a Catholic Scholars program might look like. This type of program only makes sense at Catholic colleges or universities. However, there are other "Catholic programs" which would be equally viable at both Catholic and non-Catholic institutions. Many institutions already have programs which are Catholic variations on what is being proposed here. One example comes from the Catholic center at a flagship state university where an undergraduate catechist training program is already underway. Students who participate in this program hope to be volunteer religious educators at their parish after graduation and the Catholic center helps prepare them. During one or more of their college years, these students attend a series of presentations at the Catholic center that provide information about the Catholic faith and satisfy diocesan standards for the highest level of catechist certification. These presentations are in-effect mini courses, but because they are under the direction of the Catholic center, they do not qualify for college or university credit.

Students who participate in catechist programs similar to the one described here are taking active steps to provide much needed leadership in the Church. With fewer nuns available to teach as they once did, parishes need trained and committed lay people who are willing to take the lead in teaching the next generation of Catholics. These students see this need and understand the centrality of parish life, and they are willing to make an important contribution to Church life. They should be commended along with the university or Catholic center that prepared them. Furthermore, qualifying and performing as a catechist offers young adults future benefits by better preparing them for the responsibilities they will assume if God eventually blesses them in marriage with children.

Measuring Catholic Matters

The previous section suggested a number of incentives colleges and universities can adopt that would entice students to take Catholic courses that will help them in their primary academic major and perhaps in their life after graduation as well. Assessing how successful these approaches actually prove to be is an important responsibility for those who manage the college or university's mission. Generating a report each year about the number of students in the Catholic Scholars program and the number of Catholic Scholars who graduate each year is one straightforward way to get some of that data. For a university that has a Catholic Scholars program or something akin to what we have described here, tracking actual participation rates makes it possible to gauge the impact of the program and set target rates for the future. Colleges and universities would also need to understand the real impact these programs had on participating students. To do that, they would also need to do interviews and administer questionnaires.

With or without a Catholic Scholars program, Catholic colleges and universities face a larger issue: What should they attempt to measure in Catholic matters? As nearly as possible, the measures should be related to the Catholic goals of the institution. At the beginning of this essay, we specified three Catholic goals pertinent to all Catholic institutions of higher education: Catholic knowledge, Catholic practice, and growth in Catholic commitment. These goals apply generally to all students, but particularly to Catholic students. In what follows, our focus will be on the Catholic students. However, it is obvious that with some slight changes in wording or approach, measures can be devised for all significant groups of students, whatever their religious affiliation.

Rather than consider generic statistics about Catholic academic matters, we would like to continue to focus on the Catholic Scholars program we described earlier. This program allows us to highlight the type of data that would be important for a great variety of Catholic initiatives undertaken by both Catholic colleges and universities and by Catholic centers at non-Catholic institutions as well.

Yearly reports detailing both participation rates in a Catholic Scholars program and graduation rates would generate helpful "Catholic knowledge" measures among this particular segment of the student body. Information about their participation rates in weekly Eucharist on Saturday evening or Sunday would provide a measure of "Catholic practice." Furthermore, information about the extent to which Catholic scholars participate in various student activities with a Catholic hue (such as peace and justice work, volunteer service, and pro-life activities), would provide a measure of their intensity of commitment to Catholic issues.

The most difficult of these three goals to measure is growth in Catholic commitment while at the particular Catholic college or university. That is because commitment is an internal disposition. It is possible to ask about a person's disposition, but even the individual may have trouble gauging its intensity. External acts, however, can shed light on internal disposition. For example, in addition to the examples given above, a student participating in the Catholic Scholars program may choose to volunteer in the either the local parish or in his or her parish during the summer months. Now, it is possible that this new involvement is merely a way to enhance a resume or an opportunity to spend time with a friend who is volunteering and has nothing to do with increased "Catholic commitment." However, this external sign can also reasonably be interpreted as an intensification of commitment to the Catholic faith that was brought about my participation in the program. Some qualitative data gathering will help determine what is really going on. It is somewhat complicated to collect data about Catholic commitment, but it is possible.

Measuring the impact that some type of Catholic Scholars program might have will provide some important information, but a more expansive metric is desirable. Catholic colleges and universities should try to make sure that most of their Catholic graduates have a greater understanding of the Catholic faith than they did when they entered. In order to do this, these institutions have to have a way to measure what they know when they enter and what they know about Catholic matters when they graduate. One way to make this happen is for a group of Catholic colleges or universities that are geographically dispersed (so that for the most part they are not directly competing with one another for students) but have similar missions to set a process in motion. They can appoint a steering group to make recommendations for establishing a variety of measures. As a norm to focus their efforts, the steering group could be given a maximum amount the group of universities would be willing to spend on developing the measures, gathering the data, and then evaluating it.

As indicated above, in our judgment anything like the Catholic Scholars program we describe here requires a number of faculty members who are informed, practicing Catholics. By "informed" faculty we mean Catholics who are familiar with at least some of the Catholic themes which relate to their academic disciplines. Faculty members teaching Catholic theology are clearly informed. However, a Catholic scholars program envisions courses in specific academic majors or areas which treat significant Catholic themes. Someone treating Catholic issues in the sciences would have to be well informed on scientific matters and also have some knowledge of Catholic teaching. Failing this, the course would have to be jointly taught by a well informed scientist and someone generally knowledgeable about science and very familiar with Catholic teaching in matters pertaining to science.

Consider a Catholic Scholars program that attracts 25 percent of the undergraduate student body. Assume that Catholic Scholars, in addition to required Catholic courses (theology and philosophy), take six of their courses in Catholic areas.[13] Furthermore, assume there are only two required courses. For simplicity, one can think of freshmen taking a required "Catholic course" each semester of freshman year. After that, assume that Catholic Scholars take one "Catholic course" (including those Catholic courses in their major) per semester. Thus, Catholic Scholars take one "Catholic course" per semester throughout their four academic years. More specifically, 25 percent of the student body takes one Catholic course per semester and the remainder of the student body takes the two required Catholic courses only in their freshman year.

If the norm is that students take five 3-credit courses per semester, they take 40 courses during their four years. Catholic Scholars (25 percent, we assume) take a total of 8 Catholic courses while all other students (75 percent) take only two Catholic courses during their four academic years at the institution. Finally, if students are to gain insight into Catholic teaching pertinent to their academic major, it is important that the faculty member imparting that information be well informed on the pertinent Catholic material and can interpret the material out of lived practice of the faith. For this reason, we assume that Catholic courses are taught only by informed, committed Catholics. Given these assumptions, 10 percent of the courses taught per year would have to be taught by informed, committed Catholics.

The number of informed, committed Catholic faculty members required to teach these courses depends on how specialized Catholic faculty are in Catholic courses. If one assumes half of their courses are Catholic courses, 20 percent of the faculty would have to be informed, committed Catholics. If their percentage of Catholic courses is lower, the required percentage of faculty who are informed, committed Catholics is higher than 20 percent. At the present time, many Catholic institutions would not have sufficient informed, committed Catholics to teach the courses. Those which have a good percentage of Catholic faculty members may not have a sufficient number located in the various majors in which Catholic scholars are expected to take at least two Catholic courses.

As important as this small group of informed and committed Catholics is for Catholic identity, it is most unlikely that other faculty members would defer to them when developing academic policy regarding important Catholic matters. In order to make sure its program remains strongly academic and Catholic while it informs a good percentage of its student body about things Catholic, a Catholic university requires a significant number of Catholic faculty who are committed to supporting the Catholic project on campus.[14] *Ex Corde Ecclesiae* stipulates that at least 50 percent of the faculty be Catholic and the corresponding norm applicable in the United States says that each Catholic university should strive to appoint a majority of Catholic professors.[15] Our approach focuses on how to get from here to there. In our book we argue at length that it is very important to have a cadre of committed, informed, Catholic (CICs) faculty members who assume primary responsibility for the Catholic mission, and we also outline the types of financial resources required to train such a cadre of faculty.[16] They need to be supported by a group of other Catholic faculty members who endorse and promote this mission. Their promotion of the mission occurs mainly by supporting the initiatives of the more tightly defined group of committed, informed, Catholic members of the faculty.

Catholic Impact on Alumni

Up until this point we have emphasized the importance of data in helping administrators fulfill their responsibility to educate and motivate students in the Catholic faith during their undergraduate years. To be sure, this has implications for faculty members themselves, a point to which we will return later. At this point, we would like to explore the implications of the two additional Catholic goals which most Catholic institutions of higher education set for themselves. The first of these goals is to produce leaders in society and the second is to offer an education which is valuable for a lifetime.

To the extent that colleges or universities take seriously their commitment to produce leaders in society, they have some obligation to determine at least to their own satisfaction that, over the years and for the most part, this is happening. In fact, if the institution is at least partially successful in attaining this goal, they have great incentives to share this information with alumni and prospective students of the university. All other things being equal, a university which truly produces leaders and can demonstrate it does so in a convincing manner will perform better than a university which either does not produce leaders to the same extent or lacks convincing evidence of their actual success in this endeavor.

Catholic colleges and universities with aspirations to produce leaders have an implied commitment to produce not only leaders in secular society but also leaders for the Catholic Church. In saying this, we are not implying that the Catholic college or university which produces the most cardinals or bishops is at the forefront of Catholic education. After all, there are many different types of leadership in the Church and it exists at many different levels. What we are saying, however, is that at the very least, a Catholic college or university should have some notion of what constitutes leadership in the Catholic Church.

Defining "leadership in the Church" is a task for each Catholic college or university to specify. Nevertheless, it might be helpful to offer some suggestions about what Catholic leadership might mean. Each college or university can have a slightly different approach, but each should at least be clear about what that approach is. There are two general areas of leadership in the Church. One is internal to the Church and consists in the performance of specifically Church activities at the parish, diocesan, or supra-diocesan level. The second way a Catholic can exercise leadership pertaining to the Church is by supporting Church teaching in both word and deed within the larger secular culture.

A leader rarely emerges in a short period of time, suddenly appearing, as it were, ready to lead. A leader learns skills, becomes accustomed to serving in various roles and perhaps directing smaller groups. Emerging leaders are gradually given greater responsibility over people as well as tasks. In Church matters, the roles and tasks usually begin at the local level, within a parish setting. Certainly, any college or university that produces an above average number of priests or religious women or men can claim to generate Church leadership. However, in this day and age lay people are providing most of the non-sacramental services once provided by priests, or religious brothers or sisters. Catholic colleges and universities committed to leadership, therefore, should be expected to generate an above average number of graduates who play significant roles at the parish level, at least in their initial years after graduation.

Ideally, Catholic colleges and universities should have programs to encourage their Catholic graduates to become involved with their local parish. Specifically, the college should present an ideal for recent Catholic graduates. Thus, the ideal Catholic graduate should register at his or her local parish, attend Mass weekly there, volunteer for something in the parish, and contribute financially to the operations of the parish. Leadership requires engagement, and these are the way a Catholic graduate becomes engaged in a parish. Different types of Catholic universities may have varying ideals, but, whatever the ideals are, they should be communicated to graduating seniors.

Catholic colleges interested in parish engagement should then design appropriate measures to determine whether their goals are being reached. Data for students who graduated in the least ten or fifteen years at such institutions should show an above average number serving as lectors, extraordinary ministers of the Eucharist, catechists or religious educators, ushers, members of social outreach groups, the altar society, or other parochial societies. Even if a university were above average in terms of the participation of younger graduates in only one or two of these groups, they could legitimately claim some prowess in preparing leaders for the Catholic Church.

As alumni/ae become more experienced, they have opportunities to serve the Church in more significant ways. They may participate on parish councils, in diocesan committees, national task forces, or undertake projects which in special ways contribute to the well being of the Church and the promotion of the gospel. Measuring such participation may be challenging because of the great variety of opportunities for service and leadership. Nonetheless, gathering some data and then reflecting on it is important.

In many Catholic colleges and universities, an alumni affairs unit within the institution already gathers data from alumni. They administer occasional alumni surveys, usually to classes celebrating significant anniversaries of their graduation. Such surveys could be expanded to include questions concerning Catholic (as well as generally more religious) practice and commitment. Questions concerning the knowledge and understanding of Catholic doctrine are more appropriate around the time students graduate because the information sought concerns the extent to which students acquired this knowledge through the faculty and programs at the Catholic institution they attended. With respect to practice and commitment, useful data can be collected about a variety of issues pertinent to Catholic practice and commitment. Such information would, of course, be anonymous and solicited on a purely voluntary basis. Given these parameters, the survey could include questions about material which would normally be considered private or at least known only to a small group. Questions to the alumni/ae might explore the frequency of Mass attendance, marriage status, volunteer activity in the parish, volunteer service to the poor or disadvantaged, etc. The questionnaire itself would convey important information to alums. It would indicate that the institution considers such information important and relevant to the fulfillment of their mission as a Catholic institution. In addition, some of the results of the survey might be made available to the alumni through the alumni magazine. Alumni might be encouraged to communicate their thoughts on the results of the survey. Administrators would also have the benefit of seeing the data for all the institutions in the survey. This would assist them in determining what changes to make to improve the durability of the Catholic education offered at their institution.

An issue which is addressed casually in conversation is whether Catholic institutions of higher education are less effective today than they were prior to the 1960s. Many people are inclined to believe that for Catholics the pre-1960s were golden in comparison with what came after the 1960s. Strangely enough, however, we have little data from universities that could justify any particular stance on this issue. Data exists showing greater regular participation in Sunday Mass prior to the 1960s than after the 1960s. However, we don't know whether Catholics who attended Catholic college prior to the 1960s are or were more faithful in attending weekly Mass than those who followed them.

Measures for Trustees

Trustees do not administer a college or university. Rather, they govern or oversee those who do. Their fiduciary responsibility is to make sure that the university performs the activities for which it was established as a university. For Catholic universities, this means the trustees have to make sure not only that the academic mission is being carried out but that the institution is in some appropriate way serving the Catholic Church. At the very least this means, they have a solemn responsibility not to approve policies which tend to work contrary to the Catholic Church.

The manner in which the trustees fulfill this fiduciary responsibility is by making sure that there are effective people in place to fulfill the central functions of the university, by monitoring these individuals, and by approving the general policies which promote both the academic and religious mission of the Catholic college or university. In order to fulfill these responsibilities, trustees need good data about what is happening at the university.

One common way, though very partial way, in which trustees carry out their duties is by reviewing the annual budget as well as the multi-year budgets for the next several years. They also make sure the institution has sufficient insurance and can handle any legal challenges that arise. As important as these duties are, they address necessary conditions for running any acceptable university. These types of review do not fulfill the primary responsibility which trustees have. Reviewing and approving budgets, monitoring past financial performance, evaluating the exposure to risk, and establishing policies with respect to reserves to handle adverse events are sensible steps to insure the ongoing financial viability of the institution.

All collegiate and university trustees must also make sure the academic mission of the institution is being fulfilled. For this reason, they review issues relating to faculty and students. Trustees at Catholic colleges and universities have the further responsibility of making sure the university is promoting the Catholic mission of the institution. There can be a variety of Catholic missions, but as we noted above, any Catholic mission at a university includes some instruction in theology plus usually a concern to generate a sufficient number of Catholics who actively engage in Church activities.

Some Catholic institutions aspire to national prominence in their academic achievement as well as in their service to the Catholic Church. That is, they want to be a resource to educate Catholics and other students from across the United States. The group that determines the religious thrust of the college or university was the original founding religious body. Now commonly referred to as the religious sponsors of the institution, these religious bodies have entrusted much of the responsibility for directing the college or university to the board of trustees. In some cases, the sponsors themselves have reserved powers. Sponsors with reserved powers practically always reserve some power over the Catholic mission of the institution. In particular, they do not want the trustees to decide to drop the Catholic mission of the institution. Another type of power which some sponsors reserve to themselves is the approval of the person selected by the trustees to be president of the institution. Usually reserved powers only become binding in unusual circumstances. Practically speaking, trustees specify the religious mission of the institution. The actual goals the trustees set determines the type of data they need to assess how effectively they are achieving those goals.

Catholic colleges and universities that aspire to having a national impact prepare their students to make a significant mark on the U.S. culture and polity. Such universities also aspire to make greater contributions to the Catholic Church both through their graduates and also through the services they offer at their college or university.

With respect to the students, Catholic universities with a national mission should have more extensive programs to insure that their graduates are prepared to exercise religious leadership in their local, regional, or national community. With respect to services, the larger colleges or universities may have special research institutes which explore issues of vital importance to Catholic teaching or practice. Gauging the impact of such institutes is difficult. The president is the person who, among other tasks and acting on behalf of the other officers of the university, assists the trustees in getting the information they need to fulfill their responsibilities. Hence, it is the president who usually provides information to the trustees that measures the operations of such research institutes and gauges their national impact. The president at these types of institutions also provides trustees with whatever information they need to determine whether the university is accomplishing its goal with respect to leadership in the broader community of the Catholic Church.

Objections

Because religion deals with belief and internal commitments, and because it involves the orientation of the whole person, many people are either opposed or reluctant to collect data which, at best, provide partial measures of religious participation. Many campus ministers, for example, are opposed to counting the number of people attending various religious functions, especially Saturday evening of Sunday Mass. They see these efforts as drastically reducing the scope of religion. The fact that once or twice a year dioceses regularly tell pastors to count the number of people attending Mass and submit the numbers to the diocesan offices is of little consolation to campus ministers opposed to "people counts" at Mass.

Another objection relates to the type of counting which should be done. Some argue that the number of students who participate in programs promoting social justice is the pertinent measure. We disagree, even though it does make good sense to estimate the impact of these programs by gathering data. In fact, according to Catholic teaching there should be a close relationship between social justice and an active religious practice which reinforces the promotion of justice. In one of Pope Benedict XVI's talks during his visit to Brazil, the Pope insisted on this connection. He said: "Where God is absent—God with the human face of Jesus Christ—these values fail to show themselves with their full force, nor does a consensus arise concerning them. I do not mean that non-believers cannot live a lofty and exemplary morality; I am only saying that a society in which God is absent will not find the necessary consensus on moral values or the strength to live according to the model of these values, even when they are in conflict with private interests." The Pope clearly wants Catholics engaged in promoting a more just society, but he also wants Catholics to promote that justice as they maintain contact with God in their parishes through the human face of Jesus, experienced above all in the Eucharist.

Perhaps the most sensitive objection to gathering data of the type outlined above is, in order to determine which faculty can participate in teaching students in the Catholic Scholars program, one has to intrude in the personal sphere of faculty to determine how well informed they are on Catholic matters and whether they are practicing Catholics. However, these characteristics are important because they are closely linked to distinguishability and inheritability, the two necessary conditions for any institution (Catholic institutions) to distinguish itself from other similar (non-Catholic) institutions. Catholic knowledge and commitment in a core group of faculty members is what enables the Catholic university to be distinguishable from other universities in its core academic activity. When something which is essential to an institution's identity is at stake, people of good will can find appropriate ways to gather the pertinent information.

Conclusion

Catholic colleges and universities have made many important adjustments over the past 50 years, many of which have been contributed to their survival as institutions of higher education. This paper argues the Catholic institutions must continue to make adjustments and focus in particular on the "Catholic numbers." Numbers are not everything, but they enable both faculty and administrators to better fulfill the mission of their institution and to profile more clearly its Catholic character and identity.

Melanie M. Morey has worked in the field of education and administration for the past thirty years. She received her B.A. from Smith College, an M.A. in Religious Education from Boston College, and a Masters in Educational Administration from the Harvard Graduate School of Education. Since receiving her doctorate in Higher Education Administration from Harvard in 1995, Dr. Morey has worked primarily as a researcher and consultant to Catholic colleges and universities and religious congregations around issues of governance, sponsorship, leadership, institutional identity, and Catholic culture. She is the Senior Director for Research and Consulting at NarrowGate Consulting, a division of the Catholic Education Institute.

John J. Piderit, S.J., is the President of the Catholic Education Institute. For most of his professional life, he has been involved with educational institutions of higher education. After completing theological studies in Germany, Father Piderit secured an M.A. in Economics from Oxford University. From 1978 until 1990, Father Piderit taught international economics and statistics economics at Fordham University. In 1990 he moved to Marquette University, where he served as Corporate Vice President. From 1993 until 2001, Father Piderit was president of Loyola University in Chicago. In his current position as president of the Catholic Education Institute, Father Piderit has explored new approaches to Catholic education and formation. He created a unique Catholic after-school program for children at the elementary school level in the archdiocese of New York. With Melanie Morey, he established NarrowGate, the research consulting division of the Catholic Education Institute.

Endnotes

[1]This study gathered data from 124 senior administrators from thirty-three Catholic colleges and universities about the import and impact of their institution's Catholic identity. Descriptive data from that study informed the book we authored; *Catholic Higher Education: A Culture in Crisis* (New York: Oxford University Press, 2006).

[2]See Morey and Piderit (Oxford, 2006), 114-116.

[3]Some of these placements exams are taken when students sit for the SAT and ACT exams in specific subject areas. Many students also take AP exams.

[4]See R. R. Reno, "Theology After the Revolution," *First Things*, 173 (2007), 15-21.

[5]Developing such an array of such foundational courses would reverse some of the academic specialization underway since the 16th century. William Clark provides a careful analysis of this trend in *Academic Charisma and the Origins of the Research University* (Chicago: University of Chicago Press, 2006).

[6]An undergraduate course with this title is offered every second year at Harvard University.

[7]Some topics, such as ethics or the history of philosophy, were actually taught divided in two courses. If there were two such double courses in the list provided in the next sentence, ten courses would be required in all, which is the standard number of courses required in a modern academic major.

[8]Conceptually and practically we distinguish between a Catholic Scholars program and a Catholic studies program. First, the Catholic Scholars program is intended to be open and viable for all students, whether they are in arts and sciences, business, nursing, or education. Furthermore, in a Catholic Scholars program students can take at least two "Catholic courses" in their primary academic major. For example, a student in the nursing program should be able to take a course which reviews a Catholic ap-

proach to sickness, healing, and nursing. Second, the Catholic Scholars program provides incentives for students to take more courses in Catholic theology, philosophy, and history. Some Catholic studies programs may have similar qualities, and to the extent that they do, we readily acknowledge the great help they provide to students in a great variety of academic disciplines.

[9]The Catholic Scholars program described here is a variation on the cohort model described in Morey and Piderit (Oxford, 2006). As described in this article, the program is broader than any Catholic cohort approach or Catholic studies program and it would aim to attract perhaps one-quarter of the undergraduates.

[10]Here, we use the term "students targeted by the university" because in our book we identify four different types of university (immersion institutions, persuasion institutions, diaspora institutions, and cohort institutions), each of which aims to educate different groups of students in Catholic matters in different ways.

[11]This program is consonant with John Cavadini's proposal for a pedagogy of the basics in theology. See John C Cavadini, "Ignorant Catholics: The Alarming Void in Religious Education," *Commonweal*, CXXXI (2004), 12-14.

[12]Many dioceses offer a first-level qualification and then, for those who participate in additional programs, a higher second-level achievement.

[13]The six courses proposed here would include both those general courses in theology and philosophy required of all students as well as the addition courses needed to qualify as a Catholic Scholar.

[14]If instead one-third of the students were in the Catholic Scholars program and two-thirds were in the general program, the percentage of informed, committed Catholics needed at the undergraduate level would be 6.6 percent.

[15]Article 4, paragraph 4, of *Ex Corde Ecclesiae* stipulates that "the number of non-Catholic teachers should not be allowed to constitute a majority within the Institution, which is and must remain Catholic." In the particular norms as applied to the United States the relevant section states "the university should strive to recruit and appoint Catholics as professors so that, to the extent possible, those committed to the witness of the faith will constitute a majority of the faculty. All professors are expected to be aware of and committed to the Catholic mission and identity of their institutions."

[16]See Morey and Piderit (Oxford, 2006), 331-346.

[17]Address of Pope Benedict XVI to the Latin American Bishops gathered in Aparecida, May 13, 2007, in the section entitled "Social and Political Problems." The text is available on the Vatican website.

Response to the Morey/Piderit Paper "Measuring Catholic Claims"

Very Reverend David M. O'Connell, C. M., J.C.D.

I WOULD LIKE TO BEGIN my remarks tonight by expressing gratitude to the Fellowship of Catholic Scholars for the invitation to participate in your 30th Annual Convention. I had the pleasure to appear on your program in 2002 and I am truly grateful to come before you again tonight as you consider the topic "The Idea of the Catholic University for the 21st Century."

It is a special privilege to respond to the very fine paper, "Measuring Catholic Claims" presented by Dr. Melanie Morey and Father John Piderit, S.J. I would also like to commend them on the serious work they did in their recent study, *Catholic Higher Education: A Culture in Crisis*.[1] Both the paper and the book from which it was drawn are extraordinarily well researched and well done. Congratulations and thank you both for this contribution to Catholic higher education.

When I first assumed the presidency of The Catholic University of America here in Washington some ten years ago, a long-time, very experienced trustee gave me the following advice: "Just follow the numbers, kid." It was wise counsel and has served me well over the past decade. There are many things that a university president must administer in the course of his/her service, and most of them involve "following the numbers." Our authors pointed that out—in fact, it was the starting point of their paper. They mentioned several of these "numbers:" admission inquiries, applications, enrollments, tuition dollars, and so forth. These become useful data that help university administrators measure institutional success or lack of it. I agree with their insights. I also believe that at a Catholic institution of higher learning in particular, there are many things that cannot be so easily quantified, but are no less important to measure if a Catholic institution intends to survive as such. Among these are included Catholic identity and Catholic mission, aspects of a Catholic institution's life that are not so easy for us to define in a universally accepted way, as our authors note; but we certainly "know 'em when we see 'em."

Our authors stated that "when it comes to understanding what it means for an institution to call itself Catholic, the category of Catholic identity proves not all that helpful."

Why is that the case? Some sociologists suggest that prior to the Second Vatican Council, "Catholics in the United States were treated as being different by other Americans, and, therefore, a clear identity was given to Catholics from *outside*." As demographics changed from the 1960s forward, these differences have "largely fallen down," and today's Catholics "no longer feel so distinct" or need "to defend themselves against the outside."[2] Their research indicates that while "most Catholics continue to identify themselves as Catholics," and remain so, "Catholic Church involvement is decreasing." In other words, "Church involvement is more at risk than self-identity."[3] These observations attempt to make a case that Catholic identity has been based historically on the views of those *outside* the Church—what "others" see in and about us. While there is truth, as some psychologists assert, that our identities are often largely derived from the way others view us, I suggest that there has to be something more, a fundamental, internal and real "thing"—in Latin, we use the word "*res*"—which is then communicated externally, all of which constitutes who we are even before our public reputations are established. That is what I understand by the term "identity." In the case of the Church and its institutions, I call that "Catholic identity." It is the very essence of what it means to be Catholic, whether that label be attached to an organization, a school, a university, or a hospital, and so forth.

Is the meaning of Catholic identity really that difficult to grasp, that difficult to apply to our Catholic institutions? Personally, I do not believe it is.

Pope John Paul II wrote in *Ex Corde Ecclesiae* (*ECE*)[4] of four "essential characteristics" that every Catholic university, as Catholic, "must have." They are:

> 1. Christian inspiration not only of individuals but of the university community as such;
> 2. A continuing reflection in the light of the Catholic faith

upon the growing treasury of human knowledge, to which
it seeks to contribute by its own research;
3. Fidelity to the Christian message as it comes to us
through the Church; and
4. An institutional commitment to the service of the people
of God and of the human family in their pilgrimage to the
transcendent goal which gives meaning to life.[5]

He continued:

In the light of these four characteristics, it is evident that
besides the teaching, research and services common to
all Universities, a Catholic University, by *institutional
commitment,* brings to its task the inspiration and light of
the *Christian message.* In a Catholic University, therefore,
Catholic ideals, attitudes and principles penetrate and
inform university activities in accordance with the proper
nature and autonomy of these activities. In a word,
being both a University and Catholic, it must be both a
community of scholars representing various branches of
human knowledge, and an academic institution in which
Catholicism is vitally present and operative.[6]

In 1972, long before *ECE*, Pope Paul VI remarked to the professors
and students of the Pontifical Gregorian University with respect to
Catholic identity that,

… the decisive element is a religious view of the world,
a *weltanschauung* inspired by the Catholic faith. This is
the noble and indispensable condition on which the whole
university is established and supported. And this Catholic
atmosphere, stemming from faith lived and suffered,
guarantees and respects in the university the seriousness of
scientific research rooted in man and in the human world.
On the scholarly plane an effort must be made not to break
but to enhance, scrutinize, and understand the living, vital
links with tradition.[7]

Seven years later, Pope John Paul II stated to the presidents of Catholic universities and colleges assembled at The Catholic University of
America that:

… every university or college is qualified by a specific
mode of being. Yours is the qualification of being Catholic,
of affirming God, his revelation, and the Catholic Church

as the guardian and interpreter of that revelation. The term 'Catholic' will never be a mere label, either added or dropped according to the pressure of varying factors.[8]

You wonder why this question of Catholic identity is such a problem? I think it is an oversimplification to state with sociologists that Catholics are now so well-educated and well-integrated into society that we do not feel the need to defend ourselves or emphasize our distinctness. Perhaps the problem is more basic: we have allowed ourselves to slide into a situation where we are not different or distinct or, worse, we choose not to be. Or, perhaps, we do not understand what we believe well enough to believe it or to be defined by it or to articulate it or to hand it on. Or, perhaps, within the current Catholic academic community itself—those for whom Catholic identity is important—we are more interested in arguing among ourselves or, worse, prevailing over one another—this institution is more Catholic than that one, more faithful, more deserving—than in preserving who and what we are and transmitting it to the next generation. If any of these possible explanations is true, then, more than ever our work is cut out for us in Catholic universities and colleges.

Because our authors found the expression "Catholic identity" not so easy to define or to use as a measuring tool—and they are not alone in that experience—they preferred the notion of "culture" as a way to understand and measure "the nature of institutional Catholic character and mission." While I do not disagree with that as a framework, I did not, and do not, find the term "culture" any more manageable than the terms "Catholic identity" or "Catholic mission."

By that, I simply mean that the expression "culture" itself, as commonly understood, refers to a number of realities and levels of being whose definitions are evasive and difficult to accept universally.

Our authors, however, do us a service by defining "culture" as they use the term, and, in so doing, they help focus our thinking in very specific ways: culture as a complex of present "actions" as well as "inheritances" from the past; culture as a "pattern of activity," as well as an identifiable set of content, symbols and actors; culture as that which is distinct and "distinguishable" as well as that which is "inheritable" or capable of being handed on—what theology refers to as *"traditio."* And just as Catholic tradition reflects theological development over time, so, too, the "culture" to which our authors refer also develops or, as they observe, "must be adept at making adjustments over time." I must confess that I did not find much in this paper with which I substantively disagree, so no sparks will fly in my response to it. There are, however, phrases or ideas here or there that I might present in a different way, but the paper itself is both interesting and instructive.

The topic is "measuring Catholic claims," that is, "follow the numbers, kid." And the authors have reached into their vast research to see where and how such measuring takes place and to where and how to evaluate its significance.

When writing about "characteristics of Catholic higher education," our authors stated that "Catholic colleges have an *interest* in promoting Catholic belief, understanding, and practice that distinguishes them from their non-Catholic counterparts." I would be more inclined to say *obligation* or *responsibility* rather than interest. I am interested in a lot of things, but I do not necessarily always feel any urgency, and I just might never get around to pursuing them. If "Catholic belief, understanding, and practice" constitute aspects of the "truth" that a Catholic university searches for, then it is, as Pope John Paul II wrote in *ECE* both "the honor and responsibility of a Catholic university to consecrate itself without reserve to the cause of truth (*ECE*, Introduction, art. 4)." That is a fairly strong statement of what we are all about. The obligation or responsibility, more than mere "interest," should be evident in everything that we do, especially our core academic activity. That presumes that the doers are informed and knowledgeable about the Catholic faith and its inherent and integral truth. *Nemo dat quod non habet.* No one can give what he or she does not have. Sometimes the "having" is very difficult to measure and does not come to our attention until the "giving" starts to occur. And if the "giving" does not measure up, the "having" becomes a real difficult issue to confront, because the "havers" and the "givers" are the faculty we recruit and appoint and tenure.

We also should remember that those who choose to come to a Catholic university precisely because it is distinct from its "non-Catholic counterparts" have a *right* to a Catholic education that promotes the Catholic belief, understanding, and practice that our Catholic identity and mission oblige us to champion. That includes both students and faculty, those with a right to learn as well as those with a right to teach, and both fully in accord with our Catholic beliefs and practices.

Our authors made a very important point—one that I feel is often overlooked in practice on many Catholic campuses—namely that "the Catholic faith does not exist independent of the Catholic Church."

Recall the haunting "creed" of the Land O'Lakes Statement of the international Catholic universities back in 1967:

> The Catholic university today must be a university in the full modern sense of the word, with a strong commitment to and concern for academic excellence. To perform its teaching and research function effectively, the Catholic university must have a true autonomy and academic freedom *in the face of authority of whatever kind, lay or clerical external to the academic community itself.* To say this is simply to assert that institutional autonomy and academic freedom are essential conditions of life and growth and indeed of survival for Catholic universities as for all universities (my italics).[9]

For decades, many of our Catholic institutions lived by that creed, identifying the institutional Church as "external," and we all knew who and what they meant by "authority of whatever kind, lay or clerical."

Compare that notion to the one presented by Pope John Paul II 23 years later in *ECE*:

> Every Catholic University, without ceasing to be a university, has a relationship to the Church that is essential to its institutional identity...One consequence of its essential relationship to the Church is that the institutional fidelity of the university to the Christian message includes a recognition of and adherence to the teaching authority of the Church in matters of faith and morals. Catholic members of the university community are also called to a personal fidelity to the Church with all that this implies. Non-Catholic members are required to respect the Catholic character of the university, while the university in turn respects their religious liberty.[10]

And as far as "external" clerical authorities are concerned,

Pope John Paul II asserted that:

> Even when they do not enter directly into the internal

> governance of the university, bishops "should not be seen
> as external agents but as participants in the life of the
> Catholic university.[11]

Our Catholic faith and its re-presentation within the Catholic university do not exist independent of the Catholic Church. And there are measures by which that can be identified and tested that were already mentioned in *ECE*.

The paper and its major recommendations concentrated on the undergraduate experience of a Catholic university or college in an effort to measure an institution's Catholic claims. The graduate and professional experiences within Catholic higher education are also "particularly Catholic components of institutional mission." In a university such as the one in which I serve, its core mission is precisely to serve a Catholic graduate-level community. Although there is probably and commonly much more vibrancy and energy devoted to the pursuit of Catholic identity at the undergraduate level, attention also needs to be paid to measuring evidence of Catholic identity and mission at the graduate level as well. Yes, graduate students are a different audience, with different backgrounds and experiences, different expectations and different levels of maturity, but they are still a vital and important part of the Catholic academic community. They, too, are part of this "Catholic institutional culture" that must be included in our measuring. That having been said, let us turn our attention to some of the recommendations presented in the paper.

The first suggestion, addressing what the authors classify as a "curious discrepancy," is a recommendation to introduce a "'Catholic knowledge' placement examination for entering undergraduates." The authors state:

> The absence of a placement exam in Catholic knowledge
> signals that it really does not matter how much Catholic
> knowledge the students get during their high school years.
> Even if they learned practically nothing, the faculty at
> the Catholic university will accept the students and make
> appropriate adjustments in the introductory theology
> courses at the Catholic college or university.

Personally, I do not see this recommendation or the argumentation supporting it as particularly compelling. What would it really accomplish to require a Catholic placement exam of entering students? What would it prove? How much our students do not know when they arrive? It is our job to teach and to teach in such a way that students grow in their understanding, regardless of how much understanding they may already possess or lack when they show up on our doorsteps. If students are well-versed in Catholic theological or religious faith matters, then so much to the good. If they are not, then we must roll up our sleeves and get busy. More important than a placement exam for measuring Catholic claims would be a comprehensive exam as they students exit to determine if we have succeeded in "sharing and developing" Catholic knowledge in our students, if we have given them something solid and enduring to take with them.

If I were to put the emphasis anywhere in terms of entering students, it would be on placing the very best of our Catholic theological or religious studies faculty on the front lines so that these freshmen could become excited and engaged in the study of their faith. If I were to put the emphasis anywhere in terms of all our students, it would be to ensure that our faculty teaching them are not only the "best in their fields," but also the "best in their faith." Perhaps *they* should be given a placement exam!

In a recent edition of *America* magazine, Holy Cross Father and Notre Dame professor Wilson D. Miscamble wrote:

> … if Catholic universities are to navigate successfully through the difficult challenges of the moment, they must confront the fundamental issue of faculty composition and address the need to recruit a committed Catholic faculty.[12]

The second suggestion presented in our authors' paper is directly related to the issue of faculty and that is curriculum. They state that:

> The most important discipline at a Catholic university should be theology, and, indeed, most Catholic colleges require students to take one or two courses in theology or religious studies.

Those of us who teach or administer at Catholic colleges or universities—really, at any post-secondary or graduate institution—are well-acquainted with the faculty mantra that "curriculum is the prerogative of the faculty." And rightly so. That is why they were hired and that is what they do. But not exclusively so. Faculty members are not the only ones who should be concerned about this. Each with his or her distinctive responsibilities, trustees who govern and administrators who manage; faculty who develop curriculum and students who study it; even parents, alumni and donors who have supportive roles to play in our Catholic institution's growth and development—all should be concerned with the curriculum and its transmission and its nurturing of the Catholic faith.

> *Ex Corde Ecclesiae* said it well:
>
> Theology plays a particularly important role in the search for a synthesis of knowledge as well as in the dialogue between faith and reason. It serves all other disciplines in their search for meaning (art. 19)…university teachers should seek to improve their competence and endeavor to set the content, objectives, methods, and results of research within the framework of a coherent world vision…to be witnesses and educators of authentic Christian life (art. 22). Students are challenged…to deepen a Christian way of life that is authentic …(art 23)…Administrators in a Catholic university promote the constant growth of the university (art. 24).[13]
>
> And, later, in the text:
>
> The responsibility for maintaining and strengthening the Catholic identity of the university rests primarily with the university itself. While this responsibility is entrusted principally to university authorities, it is shared in varying degrees by all members of the university community…the identity of a Catholic university is linked to the quality of its teachers and to respect for Catholic doctrine.[14]

So much attention, however, has been paid to the faculty that we sometimes forget the reason we exist in the first place: so that the students receive the best education possible. As noted earlier, they are among the Christian faithful who, according to the Code of Canon Law,

> … have the right to a Christian education by which they are instructed properly to strive for the maturity of the human person and at the same time to know and live the mystery of salvation.[15]

As our authors observe:

> At the very least, a Catholic university (*must have*) some informed and trained faculty members knowledgeable about the Catholic faith who teach courses which have significant bearing on the Catholic faith.

If curriculum is, truly, the "prerogative of the faculty," then the greatest part of the burden of responsibility and accountability with respect to "handing on and nourishing the faith" at Catholic institutions of higher learning rests with the faculty. The courses should be carefully and thoughtfully created and prepared by them, properly advertised and distributed, and, most important of all, grounded in solid, Catholic doctrine, faithful to the Church and its authentic magisterium.

Our authors' third suggestion or recommendation is very appealing to me: namely, the creation and introduction of a "Catholic Scholars" program. That given the number of course credits in Catholic philosophy and theology by those of us who retain such coursework in a core curriculum, as well as and the quality and depth of those courses, high-achieving students should be given a special designation that identifies them among their peers within the Catholic academy. Many give the designation "honors" student to those who are part of their university honors programs. The idea here would be similar.

Two other areas of campus life, referred to in our authors' paper in terms of "Catholic commitment while at the particular Catholic college or university," are worth mentioning here: the work of campus ministry as well as that of student life.

The promotion of an active spiritual life outside of the classroom is essential if our universities or colleges seek to be truly Catholic. The opportunity for a full sacramental life, nurtured by an active faith development and common prayer, makes the Catholic campus, a "Catholic home away from home." Volunteer activities and other good works—though very important and commendable—are not the pastoral equivalent of growth in faith and a life of prayer in the experience of students during a significant, formative period in their lives and personal journeys. While not easy to quantify, this should certainly be evident on the Catholic campus.

Similarly, Catholic universities and colleges that present Catholic teaching in the classroom and offer opportunities for spiritual growth outside of the classroom, but do not exercise vigilance over residential campus life and other student sponsored activities, are offering an incomplete Catholic environment that does not reflect what is taught and learned or prayed about, and what the institution values as distinctively Catholic in the way students are permitted to live. Guidelines and procedures that support Catholic living in dormitories or residence halls and that are enforced are essential to the Catholicity of the institution and community. Similarly, in health care, counseling, and other services provided to students, Catholic teachings, practices and values need to be observed as aspects of the "truth" that lies at the heart of the Catholic teaching mission.

"Follow the numbers, kid"--this was good advice given to me at the beginning of my presidency. I just hope and pray for all Catholic universities and colleges that "the numbers" lead us to the realization of the need for and the *value* added by Catholic higher education and the real possibilities it presents for us to hand on what we have been given in and through the Church—the "inheritables"— in such a way that we remain "distinguishable" from and among our non-Catholic peers as well within the Catholic academic community with an identity and mission that are "measurable," and for which we are held "accountable."

May God who has begun this good work in us, indeed, carry it through to completion! Thank you!

The Very Reverend David M. O'Connell, C.M., is the 14th President of the Catholic University of America. He has a doctorate in canon law with a specialization in Catholic higher education. As President, he also holds the John Joseph Keane University Professorship. He was formerly Associate Vice President and Academic Dean at St. John's University in New York and also Interim Academic Vice President at Niagara University. He has also served as an ecclesiastical judge and canonical adviser in a number of dioceses and also as a seminary professor. He has been nationally recognized as a supporter of Pope John Paul II's apostolic constitution on the Catholic University, *Ex Corde Ecclesiae,* with a view to its full implementation within the Catholic academy. Father O'Connell is also a Consultor for the Congregation for Catholic Education in Rome.

Endnotes

[1]Melanie M. Morey and John J. Piderit, S.J., *Catholic Higher Education: A Culture in Crisis* (New York: Oxford University Press, 2006).

[2]Dean R. Hoge, "A Demographic Framework for Understanding Catholicism in America," *Seminary Journal*, vol. 12, no. 3 (Winter 2006), p. 62.

[3]*Ibid.*, p. 63.

[4]Pope John Paul II, apostolic constitution *Ex Corde Ecclesiae* , Part I, "Identity and Mission," article 13.

[6]*Ibid.*, article 14.

[7]Pope Paul VI, *Address ad moderators, doctores auditoresque Gregorianae Studiorum Universitatis*, May 13, 1972: AAS 64 (1972) 363-364.

[8]Pope John Paul II, address *Ad prope et exstantes aedes Studiorum Universitates Catholicae*, October 6, 1979: AAS 71 (1979) 1260.

[10]*ECE*, part I, "Identity and Mission," article 27.

[11]*ECE,Ibid.*, article 28.

[12]Wilson D. Miscamble, "The Faculty 'Problem,'" *America*, vol. 196, no. 6, whole no. 4784 (2007), p. 26.

13*ECE*, part I, art. 19-24.

[14]*Ibid.*, part II, art. 4, para. 1.

[15]Canon 217.

SESSION III

Catholic Studies Programs at Catholic Universities

Introduction to Catholic Studies Programs

Robert F. Gotcher

IN 1961, BRITISH HISTORIAN AND ANTHROPOLOGIST Christopher Dawson wrote a book called *The Crisis of Western Education.*[1] In it he bemoaned the cultural amnesia and chaotic nationalistic disunity of modern higher education in the West. He proposed as an antidote a systematic study of the Western, Christian cultural heritage. For the most part, the battle to preserve a classic liberal education had been lost in Anglo-American societies. Dawson believed, therefore, that one must reintroduce the fruits of Western, Christian culture as a distinct discipline, investigated historically, so that the energy and vitality of that culture could be encountered and grappled with by modern academia. The course of studies would include a study of the Christian culture, Greco-Roman Western civilization, and the autochthonic cultures of individual countries.[2]

From the Jesuit *Ratio Studiorum* of 1599 until well into the 20th century, the idea of an integrated Catholic liberal education that introduced the student to a unified understanding of creation and its relationship to God held sway in Catholic colleges and universities. From the time of Leo XIII's 1879 encyclical *Aeterni Patris*, the tendency was to use St. Thomas (preferably read in Latin) as the glue that held the Catholic intellectual life together and could ground excellence in all intellectual disciplines. For example, the Dominican

79

A.G. Sertillanges, in the early 20th century, devoted a whole chapter of his masterpiece, *The Intellectual Life*, defending that proposition:

> No metaphysic offers natural science more helpful principles of order and of higher interpretation; no rational psychology is in closer correspondence with all the discoveries of experimental psychology and its dependent sciences; no cosmology is more adaptable or readier to welcome the discoveries that have overthrown so many ancient fancies; no ethic is more favorable to the progress of human conscience and human institutions.[4]

Dawson was still somewhat optimistic that Catholic institutes of higher education had "never altogether lost sight of the medieval ideal of an order and hierarchy of knowledge and the integration of studies from above by a higher spiritual principle."[5]

That was in 1961. Clearly something has happened in Catholic higher education since then. The contemporary multiversity has become the model for many Catholic universities. The Christian heritage has ceased to be an animating center of education, or even a required subject for systematic study. Programs that emphasized the Catholic heart of the Western intellectual life began to lose that focus, as multiculturalism and absolute freedom from institutional commitments to the Eurocentric Western and Christian heritage became a core value of contemporary academia.[6] Following the Second Vatican Council (but not because of it) there was an aggressive rejection at universities and in theology departments of St. Thomas as a guiding reference point for integration of the sciences, including theology. Aquinas had left the building. In his place, at least in theology in America, Karl Rahner stepped in.

Some academics reacted by withdrawing from the university and beginning small, Catholic liberal arts colleges intentionally modeled after the classic liberal education, sometimes coupled with Great Books seminars, and also often seeing St. Thomas as the axis around which the sciences could be studied.[7] These institutions have thrived, especially recently (in the wake of the burgeoning home school movement); and this Fellowship counts among its members some of their faculties.

Others attempted to create a college within a college that reproduce a Catholic liberal education as a program at a university. This had already begun before Dawson with the General Program of

Liberal Studies, founded by Otto Bird and others.[8] These "colleges within a college" tended to move away from their strict adherence to the classic Catholic model, sometimes by faculty attrition and sometimes by administrative fiat.

Others, such as many of the members of this Fellowship, stayed at the university, and attempted informally and in their scholarship and teaching to infuse the intellectual life of the university with the spirit of the classic Catholic intellectual and cultural tradition.

By the end of the 1980s, many scholars, and not just so-called "conservatives," began to bemoan this disintegration and lack of a unified education at Catholic schools. Theologians such as Monika Hellwig looked for a reintegration of the Catholic intellectual life, although not necessarily with St. Thomas at it center. As Hellwig recalled:

> And then came the 1980s. In the Catholic universities and colleges, voices from within were asking where, in the midst of the prevailing plurality, the Catholic identity of the institutions was to be found. When all was in motion, where was the center? When every viewpoint is to be respected, by what criteria is truth to be found? On many campuses faculty and administrative groups conversed seriously, persistently, and systematically on the question of the Catholic identity of their schools. There were ongoing efforts to understand the Catholic tradition, not in its externals and organizational constraints, but in its intellectual coherence and in its spiritual and world-building thrust. There were critical excursions into the history of the church and the churches. Serious contemporary theological works were read and discussed. Those who participated in such discussions were forging a common language to deal with challenges never met before in a world that never existed before and in an ecumenical context never experienced before.[9]

As a response to the growing desire for an integrated Catholic higher education, some faculty members at Catholic universities discovered and resurrected Dawson's proposal. In the 1990s Catholic studies programs began to spring up on Catholic campuses around the country, beginning with St. Thomas in St. Paul.[10] Other universities followed, such as John Carroll University, Seton Hall, Georgetown, Gonzaga, and Rockhurst. And many more.[11]

Secular universities also began to create with ever-increasing rapidity chairs of Catholic Studies, a trend began with Dawson himself, who in 1958 was named the first holder of the Stillman Chair of Catholic Studies established at Harvard.[12] There are also several institutional attempts at influencing the secular campus culture, such as the Institute for Advanced Catholic Studies at USC, the Lumen Christi Institute at the University of Chicago, and the St. Anselm Institute for Catholic Thought at the University of Virginia.

Finally, there was at least one stealth version of a Catholic education; the Integrated Humanities Program at the University of Kansas, founded by Dennis Quinn, John Senior, and Frank Nelick. Catholic Studies programs, through flourishing, are not without their challenges and critics in university communities. Issues sometimes surface around the relationship of the program to other departments and to the university as a whole. Sometimes these tensions may be no more than traditional turf wars. Other times, however, the issues are substantial, reflecting a difference in understanding of the nature of the Catholic University and the role that coordinating disciplines, such as theology and philosophy, play in the programs.

In the two presentations that follow, we will have a conversation that includes both a sympathetic presentation of Catholic Studies at Catholic Universities and an attempt to highlight the challenges such a program both introduces and experiences in the larger university community.

We begin with Sr. Paula Jean Miller, of the University of St. Thomas in Houston, who will describe the Catholic Studies Program at the University of St. Thomas in Houston and articulate some of the rationale for the existence and organization of the program. Following Sr. Paula Jean, we will hear from Dr. John Cavadini of the University of Notre Dame, who will articulate some of the potential problems and challenges of a Catholic Studies program at a Catholic University.

Robert F. Gotcher is an Associate Professor of Systemic Studies (Theology) at the Sacred Heart School of Theology in Hales Corner, Wisconsin. He received his Ph.D. from Marquette University in 2002. His specialties include Vatican Council II, especially *Gaudium et Spes*; Trinitarian theology; Christian morality; human life and sexuality; Catholic social teachings; Catholic liberal education; lay spirituality; Franciscanism; new ecclesiastical movements; popular culture; and *ressourcement* theology, especially that of Henri deLubac. He and his wife Kathy are both secular Franciscans, and are raising their seven children in Franklin, Wisconsin

Endnotes

[1] Christopher Dawson, *The Crisis of Western Education* (New York: Sheed and Ward, 1961).

[2] One of the practical proposals was a "Specific Program for the Study of Christian Culture," written by John J. Mulloy, and included as an appendix to the book. Such a program, in a modified form, was implemented at St. Mary's College at Notre Dame, Indiana, as the "Christian Culture Program"; it was described in a second appendix by John P. Gleason.

[3] *The Jesuit* Ratio Studiorum *of 1599*, translated into English, with an introduction and explanatory notes by Allan P. Farrell, S.J. (Washington D.C.: Conference Of Major Superiors Of Jesuits, 1970). See http://www.bc.edu/bc_org/avp/ulib/digi/ratio/ratio_web.html.

[4] A.G. Sertillanges, O.P., *The Intellectual Life: Its Spirit, Conditions, Methods* (Washington, D.C.: Catholic University Press, 1987), 116-7.

[5] Dawson, p. 133.

[6] It is perhaps telling that the Christian Studies program at St. Mary's at Notre Dame begun in the late 1950s became the Humanistic Studies program. Its focus is more on Western civilization as such rather than on Christian culture. The web page says the program "examines the literature, history, and art of Western culture as an integrated whole, from the end of the Roman Empire to the present…it features a 'great books' program and pays special attention to the role played by Christianity, by women, and by non-Western cultures in the making of western civilization."

[7] *A Proposal for the Fulfillment of Catholic Liberal Education: The Founding Document of Thomas Aquinas College* (1969). See http://www.thomasaquinas.edu/about/bluebook/index.htm.

[8] Otto Bird, *Seeking A Center: My Life as a "Great Bookie"* (San Francisco: Ignatius, 1991), 73-98.

[9] Monika Hellwig, "The Survival of Catholic Higher Education," *America* (July 16, 2001), http://www.americamagazine.org/content/article.cfm?article_id=1426.

[10] Besides the undergraduate and graduate academic programs in Catholic Studies, the Center features the John A. Ryan Institute for Catholic Social Thought, the Terrence J. Murphy Institute for Catholic Thought, Law and Public Policy, and *LOGOS: A Journal of Catholic Thought and Culture.*

[11] In a 2002 article, Crisis magazine reported that, "Francesco Cesareo of John Carroll University says that his records show that there are now 32 such programs in various stages of development." Marian Crowe, "The Case For Catholic Studies," *Crisis* (Sept 2, 2002). http://www.crisismagazine.com/september2002/feature5.htm.

[12] Among them are: Dr. Russell Hittinger, Warren Chair of Catholic Studies at the University of Tulsa, Paul Griffiths, Arthur J. Schmitt Chair of Catholic Studies at the University of Illinois in Chicago; James Patout Burns, Edward A. Malloy Professor of Catholic Studies at Vanderbilt.

Catholic Studies Programs in Global Perspective

Sister Paula Jean Miller, FSE

THANK YOU FOR THE OPPORTUNITY to return to Washington, D.C., the home of my alma mater, the John Paul II Institute, and to share with you my experience of Catholic Studies.

Catholic Studies Programs, as such, were cited in *Enhancing Religious Identity: Best Practices from Catholic Campuses.* In an article published earlier in *America* (1998) by Thomas Landy, associate director of the Center for Religion, Ethics, and Culture at the College of Holy Cross, Landy states:

> While the programs may have different strengths and weaknesses, they all aspire to give students broad exposure to Catholic culture, imagination, heritage and traditions. Unlike programs that focus primarily on theology or pastoral ministry, Catholic Studies programs cast their nets more broadly. They aim to introduce students both to Catholicism's place in the history of ideas, and to manifestations of Catholic life in art, literature, music and everyday culture.[1]

Forming young Catholic leaders in Catholic faith, culture, imagination, heritage, and traditions by immersing them in the Catholic intellectual tradition as it has developed for over two thousand years in cultures around the globe, is a creative response to the challenge to integrated learning posed by John Paul II in *Ex Corde Ecclesiae* (1990). Catholic Studies Programs focus on interdisciplinary education in an attempt to combat problems that have plagued Catholic universities in the past. Deborah Ruddy and Michael Naughton of UST–St. Paul have described these as the three "disconnects":

1) The disconnection of religious identity from the life of the university;

2) The disconnection of the liberal arts from professional preparation; and

3) The disconnection of academic life from the problems of wider urban and rural communities.

Ruddy and Naughton posit that the solution to these disconnections is a curriculum that is theologically grounded, comprehensively engaged, and institutionally embodied.[2]

These disconnections within the educational institution (ironically named a *uni-versity*) in large part occasioned Pope John Paul's apostolic constitution, whose purpose was to exhort Catholic Universities to renew their mission at a time when education, like other service industries, had become highly specialized and fragmented. His call was not to reduce the Catholic educational approach to uniformity or univocal thinking, but to challenge it to bring the rich diversity of thought, approach, disciplinal methods, and professional degree programs into a unity of truth, through a program of inter-disciplinary studies integrated by philosophy and theology.

Today, rather than presenting extensive theory behind the development of Catholic Studies Programs, I have decided instead to provide you with the elements of one concrete program, as that has been developed at the University of St. Thomas in Houston, so that those of you who are unfamiliar with Catholic Studies will have a clearer understanding of what it offers to university students. There is, however, just as broad a spectrum of Catholic Studies Programs as there are Catholic Universities, so what I offer here is just one model among many.

Any Catholic Studies Program needs to be developed in relation to the total situation of the particular university. At UST in Houston, students are required to take twenty-four credits of philosophy/theology as part of the core curriculum. We are particularly blessed with faculty in these departments who are fully in line with the Magisterium of the Church. We have the further advantage of having fourteen Basilian Fathers on campus, as well as five Franciscan Sisters of the Eucharist, along with strong lay Catholics in key administrative and faculty positions. Hence, we were not looking at Catholic Studies as an alternate approach to provide the basics of Catholicity for a "Catholic" university, as is the case for some other programs. As I've often heard our CS students enthusiastically explain, what they've learned in Catholic Studies is to "apply their theology to real life." They echo what Don Briel so clearly states:

> Perhaps as never before, the Church in the United States requires a new generation of articulate and committed young Catholics who are prepared to provide leadership in every area of public life and professional responsibility. But preparation for leadership is formed not only in the classroom but also in community living and spiritual formation.[3]

Secondly, UST is a fairly small university with approximately 1500 full time undergraduates, is situated in the Southwest "Bible Belt," and is essentially tuition-dependent. These factors required a program very limited in both financial and personnel resources, with a part time director, and faculty willing to donate their time and expertise to the project.

We began to design our Catholic Studies Program by looking to a statement on the application of *Ex Corde Ecclesiae* to the United States:

> The university shall develop and maintain a plan for fulfilling its mission that communicates and develops the Catholic intellectual tradition, is of service to the Church and society, and encourages the members of the university community to grow in the practice of the faith. (Art. 5)

A program that would enhance UST's mission as a Catholic University in Houston, Texas—the gateway to Central and South America as well as Mexico—somehow needed to focus on both the multi-disciplinary and the multi-cultural aspects of the Catholic intellectual tradition. We set out to develop a program that would help students to discover the incarnational nature of the Catholic faith within the art, literature, music, and history of various cultures, while preparing them to live their lives and professions supported by the breadth and depth of the Catholic tradition. Methodologically and financially, we wanted to capitalize on already existing programs, while supplementing their Catholic dimension, i.e., service learning, faculty-student research projects, and study abroad. Our program description reads:

> Catholic Studies is an interdisciplinary academic program of the University of Saint Thomas, open to all students. The Catholic Studies curriculum provides students with the tools to discover a particular vision of human life in

relationship with God through Christ, embedded within the intellectual, artistic, and cultural contributions of the global Catholic community. Faculty and students cooperate in learning projects that explore, enhance, and transmit the Catholic tradition incorporated within the arts and sciences for over two thousand years. The program co-sponsors campus-wide and public activities of a cultural and research-oriented nature, service learning, study abroad, communal prayer and community experience.

The three pronged purpose of the UST Plan includes:

- Academic Programs that incorporate the Catholic intellectual tradition in a Bachelor of Arts degree and in a concentration for a Master of Liberal Arts degree.
- Service to Church and Society through student service learning and internships in Houston parishes and diocesan agencies. We also determined to establish an annual Miller lecture series in honor of our president, then Archbishop J. Michael Miller, CSB, Secretary of the Congregation for Catholic Education, later named archbishop of Vancouver. The purpose of the lecture series is to extend Catholic Studies to the greater Houston community through experts in the professions who have successfully overcome the dichotomy between faith and life.
- Practice of the faith at UST by providing faculty development seminars, study abroad to centers of Catholic culture like Rome and Jerusalem, campus-wide liturgical and para-liturgical functions in which the students are able to express the relationship of the faith to their disciplines, and a living-learning residential community whose purpose is the integration of faith-academics-life.

The Catholic Studies Major—either Joint (30 hours) or Double Major (36 hours)—for the undergraduate degree requires:

- Five interdisciplinary core courses.
- Five (or seven) electives from four (or five respectively) disciplines.

The Catholic Studies Minor requires:

- Three interdisciplinary core courses.
- Three electives from three disciplines.

The Master of Liberal Arts Concentration requires:

- Three interdisciplinary core courses on the graduate level.
- Three electives on the graduate level from three disciplines.

All degree programs provide:

- Service learning / internships / community leadership experience.
- Opportunities for communal prayer.
- Study Abroad in places of Catholic culture.
- *Alpha Tau Omikron Omega* (nationally registered Catholic Studies Honor Society).

By intentionally integrating the Catholic intellectual tradition with education, the social and natural sciences, international studies, communications, business, modern languages, the arts and humanities, a degree in Catholic Studies seeks to provide young professionals in a global culture with the necessary resources to begin to "renew the whole temporal order" as taught by *Christifideles Laici.* To this end, the motto of our Catholic Studies Program invites students to *Link your profession to your faith* and so work to overcome the separation of faith and life.

Learning from Don Briel's Catholic Studies Program at "UST – North," we knew that the success of the program would depend upon the formation of a critical mass of faculty committed to both its catholicity and its interdisciplinary nature. Initially our program only existed because of the generosity of faculty who volunteered their time to provide lectures within the CS core courses, in which they presented the intersection of the Catholic faith with their respective disciplines. The result was that while students were being provided with a multi-disciplinary, multi-cultural understanding of their faith, professors did not have a similar opportunity on their peer level. For the program to be strengthened, we recognized that faculty needed that opportunity.

In June, 2007, UST invited Don Briel to facilitate the first faculty development workshop for twelve members of the CS faculty advisory committee and administrators. This seminar enabled a core group from twelve different disciplines the "leisure" of time to discuss with one another the areas of strength and weakness of Catholic education at UST, as well as ways that they could support and interact with one another across the campus.

Over the seven years of its existence, five strong core courses had been developed for the CS program, but we were still dependent upon elective offerings from other departments. These varied widely in their integration of Catholic content. The primary question tackled by workshop participants was the specification of *criteria* for Catholic Studies courses, with elective courses particularly in mind. The final document developed by the group states:

A Catholic Studies course:

- Combines and orchestrates within a sustained conversation
  a) the search for an integration of knowledge,
  b) a dialogue between faith and reason,
  c) an ethical concern, and
  d) a theological perspective—drawing the course content into vital relationship with the Catholic intellectual tradition (*Ex Corde Ecclesiae* #15-19).
- Draws explicitly upon revelation, Church doctrine, and disciplinary claims in order to investigate major issues in the discipline   (*Ex Corde* Ecclesiae #1).
- Explores the proper order of relationship between nature, man, and God within a framework of a coherent world view (*Ex Corde Ecclesiae* #2).
- Affirms the dignity of the human person as created in the image and likeness of God, restored in Christ, and sanctified in the Spirit (*Ex Corde Ecclesiae* #5).
- Demonstrates the prophetic witness of the Catholic faith for understanding and resolving contemporary problems (*Ex Corde Ecclesiae* #32, #48).

These criteria are, first of all, to be met within the five Catholic Studies core courses:

Mapping the Catholic Cultural Landscape
Philosophical and theological tools for interpreting the Catholic vision of the person in creation and culture.

Exploring the Catholic Tradition
Central mysteries of the faith in scripture, liturgy, patristics, traditions, life choices, research, and service.

Opening to Transcendence: Rediscovering Symbol
Theological insights in literature and the arts.

Connecting Catholicism with the Sciences
Principles for the encounter of theology and the sciences.

Catholic Impact in the Professions
Individual research / integrating seminar / professional internship.

These criteria are to provide a framework to re-examine and

evaluate currently listed CS electives with the UST faculty who have offered them under the previously published, more general guidelines, which cross listed courses fulfill one of the following criteria:

- Explores subjects, themes, or questions within the discipline which are expressive of and/or pertinent to specified principles and teachings of the Catholic tradition.
- Relates Catholic thought to unresolved questions or debates in the discipline, or by analyzing alternative perspectives in light of magisterial teaching, in order to develop skills in critical thinking and appraisement of contemporary scholarship
- Mentors individual research on the Catholic tradition in regard to the subject matter of a given elective.

The perennial question of students and parents regarding Catholic Studies concerns opportunities for employment and future careers. Most of our CS graduates have gone on to graduate schools in a variety of disciplines, and it is these programs that will provide the immediate preparation for professional involvement. However, some of our graduates have completed their studies or engaged in the workplace immediately after departure from UST. Some of them have reflected upon the value of Catholic Studies thus far within their experience. I conclude with their thoughts:

—In bringing me to an ever-deepening recognition of my role as steward and servant leader, and in raising my awareness and appreciation for various modes of inculturation of the faith, Catholic Studies has allowed me to better serve in the Houston metropolitan area as District Executive of the Boy Scouts of America.—Tim Caruthers, 2003.

—CS helped me to integrate my core discipline of theology into more than just an intellectual study but into a Catholic understanding of the world and a way of life. As a religion teacher, I apply my study of CS everyday as I strive to help my students integrate Catholicism into their whole way of living.—Rachael Valka, 2003.

—The Catholic Studies program prepared me for the "what's next" in my life. As a seasoned career woman who was in it for herself, climbing the corporate ladder, sacrificing all for financial and other success markers, I came to the realization that it was time to focus on my spiritual life. Through the Catholic Studies program, I had the luxury to study my faith in a deeper and broader perspective, including various courses of church history, Christian literature, and religious art. I also was able to work on myself and wake-up my latent Catholic behaviors. —Mary McGivern, MLCSP, 2005.

Sister Paula Jean Miller, F.S.E., is a member of the Franciscan Sisters of the Eucharist, and is the Director of the Center for Catholic Studies at the University of St. Thomas in Houston, Texas. She is the author of *Marriage: The Sacrament of Divine-Human Communion* (Franciscan Press, 1996) and the editor of *Mapping the Catholic Cultural Landscape* (University of St. Thomas, 2002).

Endnotes

[1]Landy, Thomas M., "Catholic Studies at Catholic Colleges and Universities," *America* (Vol. 178, No.1, January 3, 1998, 12-17) 12.
[2]Ruddy, Deborah and Michael Naughton, *Perspectives* (Center for Catholic Studies, University of St. Thomas, St. Paul, Minnesota, December 2003) 19.
[3]Briel, Don, *Perspectives*, December, 2006, 7.

Catholic Studies?
A Cautionary Note

John C. Cavadini

I WANT TO SAY AT THE OUTSET that I am against Catholic Studies departments or programs at Catholic universities and colleges. I also want to say that I do not mean to impugn the good work of anyone working in or promoting such programs. I know very well that all politics are local and that in any number of given local circumstances, this may be the best solution. So— I am not campaigning against the abundant good that I am sure is being done in these circumstances. But I am raising structural objections which I think bear on the long-term prospect for the shape of Catholic education.

I have arranged my presentation in a series of questions oriented towards thinking for the long term, hopefully not eschatologically. But my answers, just in case, are suitably apocalyptic.

First Question: What is Theology? It is:
- Faith Seeking Understanding" (St. Anselm and others).
- The Science of Faith" (Pope John Paul II, *Fides et Ratio* 101).
(Cf. "The chief purpose of theology is to *provide an understanding of revelation and the content of faith."*)
- The Science of God, or the truths we know about God put into system" (John Henry Cardinal Newman, *The Idea of a University*, Discourse III.7).
- "*Sacra doctrina*" (Thomas Aquinas, *Summa Theologica*, I.1.1).

As such, theology is essentially distinct from "the study of religion" or of any particular religion as a cultural artifact or phenomenon, though it will incorporate such study. The formal object of theology is God, from the perspective of revelation.

Accepting such a discipline at a university is not simply accepting one discipline among others. A university community which accepts in its midst a Theology Department is not different simply because it accepts one more discipline than the secular universities do. In accepting that discipline, it is not just adding something on to a paradigm already in place, but is actually accepting a whole different paradigm of the intellectual life from that of the secular universities, a paradigm of intellectual culture as a dialogue between faith and reason. Having a Theology Department means accepting a commitment to the intellectual life as oriented towards and "understanding" of something transcending all the disciplines. The openness to that transcendent mystery, beyond all of the disciplines, affirms them all but keeps each one from closing in on itself as though the "truths" it discovered were incommensurable with the truths discovered by other disciplines. It is an openness to a conversation which necessarily transcends each discipline but is not simply "interdisciplinary."

If the disciplines converge at some point, it must be at a point "above" them all, in a discipline which has as its explicit object of study the mystery which transcends all other objects of study—otherwise you are in the position either of forcing non-disciplinary solutions onto the disciplines (offering faith as an adequate scientific answer) or of declaring that knowledge is necessarily shattered into shards of truth which are absolutely incommensurate with each other. Having Theology represented as an academic discipline means, as an academic community, an openness to the idea of an integration of knowledge, and it means having the possibility of succeeding, because, in order to be truly integrative and not simply interdisciplinary, the conversation at some point necessarily becomes theological.

In this connection, it is important to observe that the "interdisciplinary" is a kind of secularized version of the ideal of "integration." Secular universities, seeking interconnections among disciplines, use "interdisciplinarity" as the rubric under which interconnections are sought. The idea catches on at Catholic universities sometimes as a substitute for "integration," a way to make it appealing to faculty members trained at secular institutions and unaware of, or nervous about, any kind of integration that might require faith in revelation. In that way, the notion of "interdisciplinary studies," or "interdisciplinarity," can be a kind of laundering mechanism, a way of laundering the true ideal of "integration" into an ideal much more easily assimilated by a faculty not formed in theological sensibilities, and so, little by little, in effect replacing the ideal of "integration" with one imported from a completely different paradigm for the intellectual life and education. Theology, from this perspective, becomes just another discipline, side by side with the others, engaging, if it is a good neighbor, in interdisciplinary conversations just like the other departments.

Second Question: Is "Catholic Studies" a discipline? In particular, what is its relation to theology?

"Catholic Studies," as I am using the term here, is the name of an interdisciplinary field of study whose academic analogues would be rubrics such as "Judaic Studies," "Women's Studies," "Asian Studies," "Religious Studies," etc. In all such cases, the question becomes, what is integrating these interdisciplinary fields? What is the principle of integration? What is the formal object of study? In "Catholic Studies," it is either "Catholicism" (or "all things Catholic") as a cultural artifact that includes a deep and varied tradition of intellectual reflection (much as Judaism does, e.g.); or it is "God as understood from the perspective of revelation" (viz., Scripture and authentic Catholic Tradition).

If it is the former, it has no way ultimately of avoiding secularization, as it is, at least formally, the study of a cultural object and has no essential methodological distinction from Religious Studies or any other Area Studies discipline. If it is the latter, it is Theology without the name, and so it will exist in a necessarily ambiguous relationship with Theology and at least an implicitly competitive relationship with Theology Departments at Catholic universities and colleges. As such, it is not simply competing for students and faculty, but is actually a competing paradigm, the paradigm drawn from secular universities where the "interdisciplinary" is the highest ideal and "integration" is unthinkable. If "theology" is taught within a Catholic studies program, there is enacted a proximate good—namely, that students are exposed to theology—but a longer term institutional threat because "Theology" is exhibited as a discipline formally incorporated under another discipline, that is, just part of the "interdisciplinary" mix. Instead of thinking of the whole university as the locus of Catholic study, or the Catholic intellectual life, where theology provides the ultimate question mark to all other disciplines, the question mark opening to a mystery beyond and above each discipline, it becomes a comma, another event in a paratactic series without any order but sequence.

Third Question: Could there be doctoral programs in Catholic Studies?

This is just another way, perhaps more provocative, of proposing the previous question regarding the identity of Catholic Studies. It is not a preposterous question, because one can get doctorates in various forms of area studies such as Religious Studies, Women's Studies, East Asian Studies, Queer Studies, etc. What would a doctoral program in "Catholic Studies" look like? If it is an authentic discipline at the undergraduate level, there is no reason, eventually, that it could not be a discipline in which doctorates are granted. What, again, would be the formal object of study? I worry that especially at this level, cultural momentum will in the long run propel this discipline towards radical secularization, much as we have seen with such rubrics as "Medieval Studies," originally Catholic and highly theological and philosophical, and now dominated almost exclusively by paradigms of cultural history which are mostly anti-religious.

Posing the question in this way also makes one think, but there is so much that would fall under Catholic Studies that it would be impossible to have a doctoral program in it! But that is just another way of realizing that the proper domain of "Catholic study" is the whole university or college, not a vacuole within it. The very fact that "Catholic Studies" is even thinkable as a discipline is because, increasingly, Catholic colleges and universities are not places where the disciplines feature any distinctive Catholic focus or perspective. But the solution to that is not to isolate this focus or perspective as its own field of study, but to work on the disciplines themselves.

On the campuses of institutions with doctoral programming in Theology, the question of the relationship between a "Catholic Studies" program at the Ph.D. level and the Department of Theology is even further exacerbated. Catholic Studies can easily become the locus to collect forms of study of Catholic culture and heritage that are more acceptable and more prestigious than is Theology to the mainline secular academy. In universities with an upwardly mobile agenda, which usually means upwardly mobile in the eyes of the secular academy, Catholic Studies will easily outcompete Theology as a dominant paradigm because it is the rubric under which non-theological approaches can be unyoked from theological questions as the organizing questions.

On the other hand, if Catholic Studies has only a weak disciplinary identity, one that does not lend itself to graduate studies and especially doctoral studies, it cannot be a rubric for long-term renewal generating an intellectual culture with resiliency and depth. For that you need a well defined tradition of reflection whose formal object is clear; and, at a Catholic university, that is inescapably Theology in the first place (conceptually at least), and, in the second place, philosophy as ordered towards theology.

Fourth Question: What is the role of local circumstances?

As I have already noted, I am fully prepared to concede that local circumstances may make the Catholic Studies rubric the option of choice for a kind of renewal of Catholic intellectual culture on campus. Perhaps a particular Catholic university has given up Theology as a formal discipline or department; perhaps there is such deadlock in the Theology Department itself that there seems to be no other way forward; perhaps there is weak leadership at the top without a sense of how to create positive institutional change without creating destructive institutional upheaval. Perhaps certain Catholic campuses have become so hostile to the idea of the integration of truth in any institutionalized way that the situation of a secular university in effect applies. It will certainly seem better that students get some opportunity for exposure to good Catholic thinking than to go without.

Still, emergency solutions are not long-term solutions, and if they are not recognized as emergency and temporary, they will, I think, ultimately subvert themselves—not in the capable hands of their current proponents, but as the years go on, and the lack of a formal object of study appropriate for an integrating discipline (namely, God) causes the field to yield to the secular paradigm of which it is ultimately (in a conceptual way) the fruit.

In my view, it is better to try to undertake the renewal of theology itself, if that is the problem. One may feel that the prospects for success are low and progress slow and the struggle hard, but that is because the questions involved truly are hard questions, and they will have to be faced eventually on the path to any deep and authentic renewal. Catholic Studies programs may be able to serve as the outer protective shells for an inner dynamic of theological renewal, but to the extent that they do in fact serve that way, I would propose that the essential and difficult questions are only being postponed. The question is whether they are being postponed productively, or in a way that makes them even harder to return to, because the secular paradigm inescapably at the heart of any rubric of Area Studies will have eclipsed the real challenge. That challenge is to create an authentic academic culture which is an unfolding of reflection from *within* a tradition, rather than simply *about* a tradition. The presence of a flourishing Theology Department, as an academic unit among other academic units, is, as I've said, a perennial question mark, prompting the whole academic culture, in its interaction with this discipline, to ask the larger question of the role of this discipline above and beyond its status as a department among others.

Catholic Studies, *qua* Catholic Studies, even if it is a hidden form of Theology, cannot do the same, because even a secular university can easily have such a department on its campus with no theoretical incoherence, just as it can have Judaic Studies with no theoretical incoherence. Only an explicitly theological paradigm for the intellectual life can provide the conceptual basis and theory for the distinctive "witness" that *Ex Corde Ecclesiae* proposes.

I close with a suggestion, instead of a fifth question. I think if "Catholic Studies" must be present on a Catholic campus, it should be thought of not as a unit of its own, implying a formal object of study, but rather somehow as a movement to encourage all the disciplines to develop in a way that has a Catholic dimension. If the name must be used, why not use it as a way of inviting the disciplines to develop such a dimension. Perhaps this means incentives such as new positions in each, or some, of the disciplines, with particular *desiderata* featured as a condition of having the position. This would have the effect of strengthening the disciplines, of strengthening the whole university as the true locus of "Catholic S tudies," and of preserving the proper relation to the discipline of Theology. It could also have the effect of bringing to campus people who have an interest in seeing the whole university develop in this direction, and in inviting the theology faculty to move in this way too. I could also see that a Catholic Studies program, understood more narrowly as an area studies program, could be a way of orchestrating and facilitating and influencing hires in other departments, if it were prepared not to have a faculty of its own and to rely on faculty from the disciplines.

Also, however, the unit would have to be prepared, in true apocalyptic fashion, to declare its task done and proclaim its own dissolution. But that is a hard scenario to envision, and a truly eschatological hope. More likely, the faculty drawn from the other units would be considered "fellows," or something of the sort, of an interdisciplinary unit, "Catholic Studies," and hence they will resist the dissolution of such a unit, that will then always exist as the "place" where things Catholic are studied, over against the whole university.

But now we have ventured into the hyper-hypothetical and it is time to quit. As I myself know too well, it is easy to make suggestions—especially for other people—and I advance this one, together with its qualifications, only as a way of provoking thought in these times of "already/not yet" in which we will always find ourselves amidst some ambiguity and tension short of the final consummation of God's purposes for this world. Thank-you!

John C. Cavadini is professor and chairman of the Theology Department at the University of Notre Dame. He is a scholar of patristic and early medieval theology, with special interests in the theology of Augustine and in the history of biblical exegesis, both Eastern and Western, as well as in the reception and interpretation of patristic thought in the West from the sixth through the ninth centuries. His publications include three books: *Miracles in Christian and Jewish Antiquity: Imagining the Truth* (University of Notre Dame Press, 1999); *Gregory the Great: A Symposium* (University of Notre Dame Press, 1996); *The Last Christology of the West: Adoptionism in Spain and Gaul*, 785-820 (University of Pennsylvania Press, 1993). His articles have appeared in such journals as *Theological Studies, Religious Studies Review, Traditio, Augustinian Studies,* and *American Benedictine Review.*

The Engagement of Catholic Universities with Secular Culture

A University for All

Christopher Wolfe

In this paper I would like to answer two questions: 1) is it possible to establish a university that is substantively in accord with Catholic ideals, but which is not formally a Catholic university?; and 2) would it be desirable to do so? The answer I will give to both questions is "yes."

I will begin by briefly looking at the idea of a university, then turn to some points from *Ex Corde Ecclesiae*, and then take up the questions I have raised.

I also want to note at the start here that, despite the fact that I am involved in a new university project, and that what I have to say today is related to my views on that project, I am speaking only for myself, and not for anyone else, either those involved in that project, or anyone else.

Truth, Catholicism, and the University

The goal of a university is the pursuit and dissemination of truth about reality. This truth is complex, as Newman notes in *The Idea of a University*. He says:

Truth is the object of Knowledge of whatever kind; and when we inquire what is meant by Truth, I suppose it is

> right to answer that Truth means facts and their relations, which stand towards each other pretty much as subjects and predicates in logic. All that exists, as contemplated by the human mind, forms one large system or complex fact, and this of course resolves itself into an indefinite number of particular facts, which, as being portions of a whole, have countless relations of every kind, one towards another. Knowledge is the apprehension of these facts, whether in themselves, or in their mutual positions and bearings.[1]

Newman points out that a university claims to teach universal knowledge, and therefore, it cannot exclude any science. If truth includes knowledge of God through reason and through faith, then theology (both natural and revealed) must be included in the university. If Catholic teaching is the fullest truth regarding God and creation that we have, then the simply best university would include Catholic theology. In fact, theology would be the "Queen of the Sciences."

Integrating truth derived from the Catholic faith would be a necessary condition for the simply best university, but not, of course, a sufficient condition. There are many aspects of reality on which Christian Revelation, and therefore Catholic doctrine, has little or nothing to say, and therefore the human sciences have a legitimate autonomy on those matters—and no commitment to Catholicism, however deep and admirable, can guarantee an accurate knowledge of the human sciences. The best university simply would integrate the truths of faith and reason.

The claim here is a radical one: not merely that universities with access to the truths of the Catholic faith are "legitimate," but rather that, if done with human excellence, they achieve most fully what the nature of a university demands that it aspire to. A substantively "Catholic" university is not merely a species of a larger genus "university." It is the full development of the nature of a university, and all other universities can be judged in relation to it.[2]

If one were to aim at establishing the very best university, then, the truths of the Catholic faith would play a central role in that university.

Ex Corde Ecclesiae and the Catholic University

For a more detailed discussion of what a "Catholic university" is, let us turn to the authoritative apostolic constitution of Pope John Paul II, *Ex Corde Ecclesiae*. In the section on "The Identity of a

Catholic University," we find this statement describing the "essential characteristics" of a Catholic University:

> Since the objective of a Catholic University is to assure in an institutional manner a Christian presence in the university world confronting the great problems of society and culture, every Catholic University, as Catholic, must have the following essential characteristics:
>
> 1. A Christian inspiration not only of individuals but of the university community as such;
> 2. A continuing reflection in the light of the Catholic faith upon the growing treasury of human knowledge, to which it seeks to contribute by its own research;
> 3. Fidelity to the Christian message as it comes to us through the Church; and
> 4. An institutional commitment to the service of the people of God and of the human family in their pilgrimage to the transcendent goal which gives meaning to life.[3]

This section goes on to point out the essential interconnection of university qualities with Catholic qualities:

> In the light of these four characteristics, it is evident that besides the teaching, research and services common to all Universities, a Catholic University, by institutional commitment, brings to its task the inspiration and light of the Christian message. In a Catholic University, therefore, Catholic ideals, attitudes and principles penetrate and inform university activities in accordance with the proper nature and autonomy of these activities. In a word, being both a University and Catholic, it must be both a community of scholars representing various branches of human knowledge, and an academic institution in which Catholicism is vitally present and operative.[4]

These points are restated at the beginning of the second part of the document, which provides "General Norms":

> § 1. A Catholic University, like every university, is a community of scholars representing various branches of human knowledge. It is dedicated to research, to teaching, and to various kinds of service in accordance with its cultural mission.
>
> § 2. A Catholic University, as Catholic, informs and carries out its research, teaching, and all other activities with

> Catholic ideals, principles and attitudes. It is linked with
> the Church either by a formal, constitutive and statutory
> bond or by reason of an institutional commitment made by
> those responsible for it.[5]

The two sentences of this last section (§2) describe two different aspects of a Catholic university, which I will call the "substantive" elements of a Catholic university and the "formal" element. The substantive elements focus on the way in which Catholic truth informs the activity of the university. The first three characteristics described earlier exemplify these qualities: Christian inspiration (of the community as well as persons), reflection in light of the Catholic faith on the growing treasury of human knowledge, and fidelity to the Christian message as it comes to us through the Church.[6]

The formal element is the bond between the university and the Church. The kind of bond varies according to the particular kind of Catholic university under Canon Law. There are three categories of Catholic universities, according to *Ex Corde Ecclesiae*: 1) those established by the Holy See, by an episcopal conference or another assembly of the hierarchy, or by a diocesan bishop; 2) those established (with the approval of the diocesan Bishop) by a Religious Institute (or other public juridical person); and 3) those established by other ecclesiastical or lay persons, which may refer to themselves as Catholic universities with the consent of the competent ecclesiastical authority (in accordance with the conditions upon which both parties shall agree). In the first category (and perhaps the second), there is a "formal, constitutive and statutory bond" between the university and the Church.[7] The Church hierarchy exercises legal governance over the university. In the case of the third category of Catholic universities, rather than a formal, constitutive and statutory bond, there is "an institutional commitment on the part of those responsible for it."

Now—moving toward an answer to the question I proposed at the beginning of my paper, as to whether a university can be substantively in accord with Catholic principles, though not formally Catholic—it appears that, according to *Ex Corde Ecclesiae*, a university needs both the substantive and formal elements to qualify, juridically, as a Catholic university. That is, a university that possessed the substantive elements, but lacked a formal juridical tie to or institutional commitment to the Church, would not qualify as a Catholic university, under *Ex Corde*

Ecclesiae.[8] It would be a university that is substantively in accord with Catholic principles, but not formally Catholic.

One consequence of the fact that the university is not formally Catholic is that such a university, even though its life would be informed by Catholic ideals and principles, would not have the right to call itself a Catholic university. Recognizing that fact would prevent attempts by a university to "have its cake and eat it too": for example, to claim, generally, that it is not a Catholic university, but then to say that it is a Catholic university when it is possible to obtain benefits therefrom (e.g., in fundraising).

Perhaps the most that such a university could say (if it wished to) is that it is a university "in the Catholic intellectual tradition."[9] (Of course, this is an interesting, but uncommon, reversal of the usual problem in contemporary Catholic university life: namely, a university making a claim that it *is* a Catholic university, but then failing to bring Catholic principles to bear consistently upon its intellectual life.)

If it is possible, then, to have a university that is substantively in accord with Catholic principles, but not formally Catholic, the next question—an obvious one—is why anyone would want to establish such a university.

Why Not Be a Catholic University Formally?

Before I give my answer to this question, I want to make the very important point that I am not saying in any way that what may (as inadequate but convenient shorthand) be called an "informal" Catholic university is superior to formally Catholic universities. I would argue that they both contain the most important substantive elements that go to the heart of what a university is: an institution that pursues and disseminates truth. The factors that might make them choiceworthy or not are matters of prudence, which depend on circumstances. In the final analysis, I would argue that both the Church and secular society are best served by there being a mixture of different kinds of (Catholic) universities.

Let me begin to approach this question by describing a reaction of mine that some of you may share. When I hear someone talk about an educational institution like Brandeis, or Yeshiva, or like Wheaton College or Calvin College, my initial reaction—the vague general impressions that spring to mind and form a context for listening to what is said about it— is a combination of a) respectfulness, since these are all educational institutions involving serious people doing serious work, and b) a sense of "distance" from them, because, as good as they are in many ways, they are ultimately committed to religious views (Jewish, Protestant) that I do not share. There is a sense that, while I may derive benefits from the work of people at these places, and I recognize the good they do for those associated with them and for society at large, they are not "for me." In the final analysis, I am in some significant way an "outsider" to these institutions.

I am not defending this attitude. Depending on the form it takes, I might even criticize it. But for the moment I am just observing it. And I believe that my reaction is shared by most others who do not share the religious commitments of those universities. Respect, perhaps, but also some distance.

On the other hand, when I think of a Catholic university, I never think of it as a "university for Catholics." I habitually think of it as a university that is blessed with resources that enable it to be the best university (at least in principle) for everyone. But, of course, on reflection, I realize that, subjectively, non-Catholics inevitably have the same reaction to it that I have to non-Catholic universities (religious or secular). From their perspective, understandably, there will always be a certain "distance" that they feel toward a university that calls itself Catholic.

I digress for a moment here to point how deeply ironic it is that non-Catholics (and, for that matter, many Catholics) do not feel the same way about secular universities, which are often regarded as places that do not have "parochial" commitments. But secular universities have their own dogmas, which are manifested in countless ways. Sometimes those manifestations are explicit, as when a Christian group on campus is persecuted for its alleged "homophobia"; or when a teacher dismisses a religious position without even attempting to give a fair statement of that position, as when the Catholic position on sex is summarized by saying that sex is only good when it produces children (an example I take from a class my daughter took at a prestigious liberal arts college). Sometimes, the impact of the secular dogmas is more subtle, as in the endless talk of diversity in universities that are dramatically lacking in religious diversity, without any apparent sense of discomfort.

Moreover, the subtle dogmatic commitments are often reflected not in what is said, but in what is not said—for example, the discussion of so many philosophical and ethical issues with little or no advertence to religious and philosophical positions (such as natural law) that have played prominent roles in the history of Western civilization. Nor are the religious examples that I have cited the only examples of secular dogmas. Environmentalism, feminism, anti-capitalism, agnosticism, different forms of "scientism"—the list is quite a long one.

At any rate, my general point is that an explicit religious commitment or affiliation (understandably, if wrongly) creates a certain mental barrier between an institution and many other people in our society. It is thought to convey a message (one Catholics would never think of sending) that this university (a Catholic university) is a university only for Catholics, and not for them. For the reasons given above, Catholics naturally tend to think of our universities as universities for everyone. We can sometimes fail to recall that we are viewed as "sectarian" or "parochial" by many others.[10] (And we do have to recognize that this is also partly due to the de facto imperfections of our Catholic universities.)

I think the point I am making—that a formal religious affiliation erects a certain kind of barrier—can be developed more by looking at it in light of a certain approach to lay spirituality. One of the key distinctions between a religious spirituality and a lay spirituality is that religious are called out of the world and "consecrated." They may remain outside the world permanently, as in the case of cloistered religious, or they may go back into the world, to preach and evangelize or to perform myriad good works (spiritual, charitable, educational). But, in a fundamental sense, they always remain "set apart" for these works. (The religious habit is a sign of that consecration.) Lay people, on the other hand, are not called out of the world to live their faith, but are called in the world, right where they are. Sanctifying the world from the inside, as leaven in the world, is their vocation. So they don't "penetrate into the various sectors of society" —because they never left it.

It is also worth pointing out that lay people have a right, deriving not from hierarchical authority but from baptism, to promote educational (and other) initiatives, in cooperation with other Catholics, and with Christians and non-Christians. And yet, if these lay people are rightly convinced that the full truth may be best pursued only within the fullness of the Catholic tradition, and they wish to establish the best university possible, then the university they seek to found cannot but be Catholic in substance, while not necessarily being formally Catholic.

Moreover, those who promote a university do so by cooperating, in some measure, with parents, who have a special duty to provide for the education of their children, which is not assigned by the hierarchy, but comes from the fact of their parenthood. This parental duty and right may be attenuated as children get older, but parents still retain a certain role in their children's university education, and this, too, provides a ground for Catholics to promote educational initiatives on their own responsibility (without the formal sponsorship of the Church hierarchy).

At the same time, it must be repeated that, since these lay people are acting on the basis of their own legitimate freedom, they must also take full responsibility for what they are doing—which means not invoking the authority of the Church for what they are doing, by calling their institution "Catholic."

One ordinary way of acting in the world for those who understand lay spirituality this way is to avoid establishing or emphasizing distinctions between themselves and their fellow citizens—distinctions, including religious distinctions, that set them apart from their fellows. Of course, sometimes their behavior in accord with their personal spiritual ideals will be different from that of others, and so they will, in a sense, "stand out," and they will not shrink from that. But they will have a predilection, in public life, for not "labeling" themselves as Catholic and confining themselves to "Catholic" groups and activities, because they feel themselves to be very much a part of the world (in the non-pejorative sense of that term, because of their love for God's creation, which he called good).[11] They will often— perhaps typically—want to collaborate in many areas with all their fellow citizens, including those of other faiths, and those of no faith.

Returning to my general point, the psychological barrier arising from an explicit religious affiliation is sometimes, I think, an obstacle to Catholic universities being more a part of the general educational and intellectual life of the nation. That is especially true for Catholic universities that have not made the compromises that most mainstream Catholic universities have made, which lower the psychological barrier by diminishing the actual substantive differences between a Catholic and a secular institution university.[12]

This "marginalization" of Catholic universities is unfortunate in at least two ways. First, it is a loss to society, since it loses the benefits of "indirect" access to those truths that can be gleaned more effectively by Catholics studying with the advantages of the parameters of the faith that protect them from certain errors. I think this topic was well covered in twentieth-century debates about "Catholic philosophy." Strictly speaking, there is no Catholic philosophy, since, if it were really Catholic, it would be theology rather than philosophy. But, in fact, it is possible to do philosophy "in light of Catholic truth" without directly relying on revelation—a form of "Catholic philosophy," in a less strict sense. The image one might think of is this: we can enter a room with the light turned on, and see where everything is. If we leave the room, turning the light off, and go back in, we can feel around and find the same things we saw earlier, with other senses. The fact that the earlier vision made it much easier to find things with the lights out does not mean that what we experience without that light is not accurately experienced and genuinely known. Of course, we have to go back in the room—with others who have not seen it in the light —and feel around and actually find the things that way.

Second, it is also a loss to us Catholics, since many non-Catholics are really smart, and we can benefit greatly by working with them. It is worthwhile pointing out here that one aspect of a university that is a university like any another, that does not set itself off, and is open to the world, is that it can avoid a too-adversarial attitude toward other universities and intellectuals, fostering a spirit of working with others (all others) to solve common problems.

Because it has not really been tried, we can only speculate at this point as to whether a university that is substantively in accord with Catholic principles, but not formally Catholic, will be able to overcome, or at least mitigate, the sense that a Catholic university is a university for Catholics, and "narrower" or "more parochial" than secular universities— those secular universities that not only lack formal religious affiliation, but also lack a genuine openness to religious questions (that have, that is, their own, typically unacknowledged parochialism). Obviously, the commitment to intellectual positions that are integral to the Catholic intellectual tradition may be regarded by some observers as making the university no different from formally Catholic universities.

But the attitude of others toward the university might be significantly affected by the way members of such a university comport themselves. To what extent do its members (especially its faculty and students) genuinely engage the key issues facing current society? To what extent do they grapple—seriously and respectfully—with a wide range of answers to various questions, including the leading "secular" positions? To what extent do they actually talk to leading secular thinkers, earning their respect by their civility, their knowledge of the issues, their ability to provide internal as well as external critiques of competing intellectual positions? (That is, to what extent do its members provide intellectual analysis of high quality, according to at least reasonable disciplinary standards, as well as standards derived from a broader framework rooted in the Catholic intellectual tradition.[13])

At this point, we have to observe another possible benefit of not being a formally Catholic university, while still bringing Catholic principles to bear on scholarship and teaching. There is a genuine danger that, in a formally Catholic university—perhaps especially one very self-consciously faithful to Church teaching—the standards of good scholarship may too easily be reduced to its compatibility with, and reinforcement of, Catholic teachings. The emphasis in evaluating scholarship may too often be placed on "how Catholic" it is. But the fact that scholarship arrives at "Catholic" conclusions, or reinforces Catholic teachings, is no guarantee that it is good scholarship. It may be poor scholarship, in fact, which reaches conclusions too easily, which overgeneralizes, which lacks a sound train of reasoning, which does not come to grips with the best empirical data (the "inconvenient" as well as the "convenient" data), which fails to note and respond to apparently plausible arguments that would lead to contrary conclusions.

My argument here, of course, is not that this will inevitably happen at formally Catholic colleges, and cannot happen at informally Catholic colleges. Of course that is not the case.Still, I think that it is less likely to happen at universities that are not formally Catholic, because of the greater emphasis there on legitimate secular standards, and that it can happen more easily at universities that are formally Catholic, because of the emphasis on "Catholicity" there.

Two Practical Concerns

There are two legitimate practical concerns regarding a university that is not formally Catholic, though it brings Catholic principles to bear on its intellectual life. One involves government regulation, the other is a matter of continuity of mission.

We can get a flavor for the first concern by looking at the *Bob Jones University* case. In 1983, the Supreme Court upheld the IRS denial of an educational tax-exemption to a fundamentalist university that explicitly discouraged interracial dating, on the grounds that a tax-exemption would encourage or facilitate something contrary to public policy (the elimination of racial discrimination). A Catholic might, in good conscience, support the outcome of that case, as a way of encouraging the desirable social goal of eliminating racial discrimination, or might oppose it, for various reasons. But, irrespective of our evaluation of that case, it is easy to see in it potentially dangerous implications for religious liberty. Religious groups that have practices frowned on by government officials or political majorities (on grounds that are plausibly non-religious) may be subject to various forms of pressure or punishment. For example, it is easily imaginable that a similar stance be taken toward the tax-exempt status of a church that refused to ordain women, or a university that was deemed insufficiently supportive of rights against discrimination for homosexuals.

Of course, the outcome in the *Bob Jones University* case demonstrates that the religious character of an institution will not necessarily protect it from hostile action. Still, I do believe that it is more likely that religiously-affiliated universities could successfully resist such attempts. This might be achieved in the courts (though *Oregon Dept of Human Resources v. Smith* has reduced the legal weapons to accomplish that), or (more likely) by obtaining legislative exemptions based on conscientious religious beliefs. At the same time, the action of Massachusetts in putting the Catholic Church out of the adoption business, by requiring placement of children with homosexual couples, is another warning that religious exemptions may be denied.

What would a university do, if confronted with, for example, a requirement of non-discrimination against homosexuals? A religiously-affiliated institution might invoke its constitutional educational rights under the First Amendment religion clauses, with some reasonable likelihood of success. But what about a university that had no formal religious affiliation and therefore could not interpose a religious objection to such legislation?

My own view would be that a university like the one I am describing should be content to accept the requirement of non-discrimination against homosexuals. The real ground of discrimination would not be whether people are homosexual, but whether they hold views that consider homosexual activity immoral. A private university could make a First Amendment speech claim that those who reject the natural law position integral to the university's mission—i.e., active homosexuals and heterosexuals who support active homosexuality—lack a bona fide occupational requirement for being hired or retained as employees of the university, and this requirement is not a function of whether they are homosexual. There is no guarantee that this will work, of course—judges and legislators sometimes are simply hell-bent on achieving a result, and don't let legal principles get in their way. But, in principle, the argument is sound, and the argument is worth making. In fact, it would be very unfortunate if all the institutions committed to traditional moral beliefs were to invoke specifically religious grounds for their policies, leaving no one to make the important argument that traditional morality is based on reason as well as revelation.

The second practical concern is how an informally Catholic university would remain true to its vision over time, without the institutional connection that a formally Catholic university has.

I will pause only for a moment to point out that the formal Catholic connection does not appear to have been a consistently effective mechanism for ensuring the fidelity of officially Catholic institutions to a substantive Catholic vision. One might even go so far as to ask whether the formal Catholic connection sometimes provides a sort of "cover" for weakening the substantive one.

The question here is really a variation of a perennial question of political philosophy: is the most effective way to guarantee good government a) having good institutions, or b) having good people? In a very general way, it can be said that classical political philosophy tended to put the emphasis on good people and modern political philosophy has tended to put the emphasis on good institutions. Kant famously said that, with the right institutions, a race of devils could have good government.[14] The American founders, too, tended to rely on good institutions, such as separation of powers and checks and balances, federalism, and so forth. For Aristotle, on the other hand, the key to maintaining a constitution was to have people with certain moral qualities that fit that constitution. Of course, neither the founders nor Aristotle thought that good institutions could work irrespective of the character of rulers and citizens, or that good institutions were irrelevant to good government.

My own view is that those who are responsible for a university have to choose people who understand and are committed to its mission and are capable of maintaining (that is, have the governing prudence to maintain) the university's commitment to that mission. In the absence of those capacities, no formal affiliation of a university is likely to preserve its essential character.

Of course, if the university is formally connected with the Church in some way, that can be a useful way of maintaining the character of the institution. It provides a formal public commitment that can be invoked by members of the community to resist temptations to back down from the implications of that commitment. But there seems to be no reason why the ethos of a university in which Catholic beliefs, principles, and attitudes are brought to bear on university life could *only* be achieved and preserved by a *formal* connection to the Church. A strong articulation of the university's *raison d'être* in its founding and governing documents, and serious attention to shaping an "ethos" of the university that reflects those principles and choosing people committed to that ethos, seem to be the most fundamental requirements—with or without a formal connection to the Church.

Conclusion

I want to reiterate, in conclusion, that my argument is *not* that the kind of university I have been describing and defending—one whose life is shaped by the Catholic intellectual tradition, though without being formally Catholic—is the "right" or the "best" kind of university. I argue simply that it is a legitimate form of university, and that is lacks nothing essential for being, in principle, at least one form of " the best university simply."

I also want to point out that this is just an outline of a different kind of university. Many of the implications for the practical policies of such an institution remain to be discussed and worked out, perhaps especially in what is typically referred to as "student life," as opposed to "academic affairs."[15]

Finally, I should also mention that my concerns in this forum, and the need to avoid unnecessarily complicated language, have led me frequently to use such phrases as "an informal Catholic university," a usage that might be misleading. For, in such a university, there would generally *not* be a great deal of talk about "Catholic principles" as such. The members of such a community (outside of discussions specifically concerned with Catholic theology) would generally talk about "truth," without adjectives, precisely in order to address themselves unambiguously to all their fellow citizens, and not just to their fellow Catholics

Christopher Wolfe is a professor of Political Science at Marquette University. He received his Ph.D. from Boston College in 1978. His books include: *The Rise of Modern Judicial Review: From Constitutional Interpretation to Judge-Made Law* (1986); *Judicial Activism: Bulwark of Freedom or Precarious Security?* (1991); and *How to Read the Constitution: Originalism, Constitutional Interpretation, and Judicial Power* (1996). In his book *Natural Law and Liberalism* (2006), he criticizes contemporary liberal political theory and argues that the traditions of natural law, as represented by Thomas Aquinas, and of liberalism, with its commitment to equality, political consent, competent limited government, individual rights, and the rule of law, are not hostile to each other but mutually reinforcing, if properly understood. Recently, Dr. Wolfe has become vice-president of the Thomas International Project and co-director of the Ralph McInerny Center for Thomistic Studies.

Endnotes

[1] John Henry Newman *The Idea of a University* Discourse III, section 2.

[2] This point is similar to the point that Paul Griffiths makes about religion in his "The Very Idea of Religion," *First Things* 103 (May 2000): 30-35 (and also the correspondence about it in subsequent issues).

[3] *Ex Corde Ecclesiae* #13 (internal quotation marks and footnotes omitted).

[4] ECE #14 (internal quotation marks and footnotes omitted).

[5] Part Two (General Norms), Article 2.

[6] But see footnote 8 below.

[7]The uncertainty about the second category arises from the fact that Article 1 § 3 seems to treat the first category as distinct from the other two: "A University established or approved by the Holy See, by an Episcopal Conference or another Assembly of Catholic Hierarchy, or by a diocesan Bishop is to incorporate these General Norms and their local and regional applications into its governing documents, and conform its existing Statutes both to the General Norms and to their applications, and submit them for approval to the competent ecclesiastical Authority. It is contemplated that other Catholic Universities, that is, those not established or approved in any of the above ways [i.e., the second and third categories - CW], with the agreement of the local ecclesiastical Authority, will make their own the General Norms and their local and regional applications, internalizing them into their governing documents, and, as far as possible, will conform their existing Statutes both to these General Norms and to their applications." But then Article 3 § 4 treats the first two categories as a unit, differently from the third category: "In the cases of §§ 1 and 2, the Statutes must be approved by the competent ecclesiastical Authority."

[8]Since I have suggested that the earlier listing of four "essential characteristics" of a Catholic university describe the "substantive" elements, I should mention one qualification. In that list of four essential characteristics, the fourth referred to "an institutional commitment to the service of the people of God and of the human family." Depending on how this "institutional commitment" is understood, it might be what I have called a substantive element (if it is simply a general commitment of service to people), or it might overlap with the formal tie to the Church (if that is what is meant by "institutional commitment").

[9]The practical difference is this: a claim to be a Catholic university asserts a relationship to the Church that requires validation by those who have the authority to say what is, and is not, consistent with the teaching of the Catholic Church; a university in the Catholic intellectual tradition makes a claim that is simply an observation about whence it draws its inspiration.

[10]In this regard I cannot help recalling lines from G.K. Chesterton's book *The Thing*, in which he comments on statements by the Bishop of Birmingham, who had said "that Indian and Chinese metaphysics are now much more important than ours," and "that Rome is thus stamped as Provincial." Chesterton's response was that "this seems to suggest to the educational mind the construction of an examination paper in elementary general knowledge. It might run something like this: 1. From what language is the word 'provincial' derived? 2. To what provinces did it generally refer? 3. If Athens, Antioch, Rome, and Jerusalem were provincial towns, what was their Metropolitan city? 4. What reasons are there for supposing that Birmingham occupied this Metropolitan position from the earliest times? 5. Give a short account of the conquest of Southern Europe and the Near East by the Emperors of Birmingham. 6. At what date did the Papacy rebel against the Diocese of Birmingham? 7. Explain the old proverb, 'All roads lead to Birmingham' . . ."

[11]I say here that they act this way in public life, but I should note that the distinction between "public" and "private" is not always clear. Family life, and by extension, early education (elementary and high school) are arguably in a sort of private sphere in which the formation of children gives more room for specifically Catholic institutions

and activities. And, as I have indicated, formally Catholic universities are certainly legitimate and desirable. I only argue that they do not preclude universities that are substantively in accord with Catholic principles, but not formally Catholic, and that lay Catholics have a right to promote them.

[12]Those compromises consist especially in adopting, discipline by discipline, the general prevailing, secular standards of intellectual excellence as the dominant, almost exclusive, standards of excellence. These compromises—plus the resources to hire people who often do very good work, by disciplinary standards— have probably played a role in leading Catholic schools (Notre Dame, Georgetown, Boston College) managing to break into the conventionally regarded higher ranks of academia somewhat. Never at the top—but at least in the conventional upper ranks. Still, it is not entirely clear whether these compromises were ever really necessary even in order to gain the respect of non-Catholics. Is the philosophy department at a leading Catholic university more prestigious because it followed the trends of secular universities? Might it have been as, or even more, prestigious if it had maintained a sort of independence and distinctiveness, for example, through a commitment to Thomism, developing it in ways that engaged the central questions of contemporary intellectual life?

[13]One must distinguish here between reasonable disciplinary standards—those that genuinely flow from analysis rooted in sound disciplinary knowledge and methodology—and ersatz disciplinary standards—the result of mere ideology. For example, to the extent that current scholarship in an area of, say, English or sociology, is shaped by post-modernist and radical feminist ideological commitments, it does not represent sound disciplinary standards, irrespective of its influence in prestigious departments or publications. For a good example of this, see James Seaton's review in the *Weekly Standard* of *The Cambridge Companion to Willa Cather* (September 8, 2007). Of course, the rejection of such ideological standards must be adequately defended by trenchant analysis of the subject matter and the defective scholarship.

[14]"The problem of organizing a state, however hard it may seem, can be solved even for a race of devils, if only they are intelligent. The problem is, given a multitude of rational beings requiring universal laws for their preservation, but each of whom is secretly inclined to exempt himself from them, to establish a constitution in such a way that, although their private intentions conflict, they check each other, with the result that their public conduct is the same as if they had no such intentions" (Immanuel Kant *On Perpetual Peace*).

[15]Without denying that there is a distinction between academic life, strictly speaking, and other aspects of student life, I would also point out that the disjunction between academic life and the rest of student life is, in most universities, much too sharp. Even the "geography" of universities is often such that "academic life" is confined to classrooms and library, and life in dormitories is almost divorced from the intellectual life.

The Catholic Authority of Reason

Michael D. Aeschliman

In 1988 Joseph Cardinal Joseph Ratzinger devoted much of his St. John Fisher Lecture at Cambridge University to a discussion and reaffirmation of the arguments made in C.S. Lewis's 1943 treatise on the Natural Law, *The Abolition of Man*. In his new role as pope, Benedict XVI attracted world attention, and hostile comment, in his autumn 2006 lecture in Regensburg, in which he deplored both the de-Hellenization of the Christian religion and the use of coercion in religious matters.

Neither C.S. Lewis nor the pope had the option of living and developing their ideas in an ivory tower in an era of peace and order. Lewis had served on the Western Front and had been badly wounded in World War I. Joseph Ratzinger had experienced the Nazi horror first-hand as a conscripted soldier at the end of the Second World War. Like his great predecessor, Pope John Paul II, he lived the confrontation with the political nihilisms of Nazism and Communism in his own homeland.

In the same apocalyptic year that Lewis delivered the lectures in Durham that became *The Abolition of Man,* 1943, a learned English Jewish émigré to the United States published a devastating critique of the ascendancy to predominant power in American public education of the "Progressive" ideology of John Dewey and his disciple William Heard Kilpatrick. The émigré's name was Isaac Kandel and his book was called *The Cult of Uncertainty* (1). Initially sympathetic to Dewey's approach, Kandel had emigrated as a mature academic from Britain to the USA to do a doctorate, and eventually to teach, at the fortress of American Progressivism, Teachers College, Columbia University, where he was to spend his own distinguished academic career as an increasingly isolated critic of the anti-intellectual tendencies that he came to see at the heart of educational "Progressivism." Richard

Hofstadter's important 1962 volume *Anti-Intellectualism in American Life* was to draw heavily on Kandel for its critique of Dewey and the "Progressives" and the effects of their experimental "cult of uncertainty" on American public schooling.

Nineteen forty-three was an unpropitious year for Western intellectual authorities to confess skepticism about the basis and reality of ethics, its rationality and coherence, and about the ordered virtues that the Classical-Christian tradition had conveyed intelligibly, with intermittent success, across nineteen centuries, by means of its shaping of families, churches, schools, and universities, as well as political and social life. As a Jew living safely in America, Kandel could not help but be appalled at the childish fecklessness of a "child-centered" naturalism in education that could in no way prepare young people to face or live prudently and decently in a world such as the world was in 1943. Even the very limited decencies of Anglo-American civilization looked like considerable accomplishments in comparison to the ferocious Nazis, Fascists, and Communists who felt no "cult of uncertainty" at all.

For the gradualist, secular, liberal or Whig ideology of collective human progress—cumulative, inevitable, irreversible—was in ruins by 1943, ruins that all could see. Its tragic, brutal utilitarian rival, Marxism, had surely waxed as it had waned, as had the neo-pagan ideologies of Germany, Italy, and Japan. In some important sense, the moral, cultural, and intellectual reverberations of which we continue to feel, "Western civilization" had come to an end. Most of its European heartlands were in the grip of hysterical, barbaric, and murderous worldviews or ideologies which would have been simply inconceivable to all but a few intellectuals or other citizens before 1914. The few prescient, nonconformist 19th-century thinkers who saw the barbarous possibilities of the 20th-century future to come deserve our memory, praise, and study: Among them were Kierkegaard, Newman, Burckhardt, and, we must add, the popes.

Through fidelity to doctrine and the renewed rationalism brought about by the Thomistic revival, the Church was able to critique and oppose the emergent ideologies and fanaticisms that were to make the 20th century apocalyptic: nationalism, Social Darwinism, Marxism, Nietzshean libertarianism, and vitalism. Richard Weikart has recently shown how only Catholics and a few Socialists were able to oppose the

Social Darwinism emergent in 19th-century Germany that contributed mightily to Nazism (2). Similarly, Richard Gid Powers's outstanding 1995 volume, *Not Without Honor: The History of American Anti-Communism* (3) valuably documents the steady, dogged, decades-long Catholic critique in the USA of Marxism and European Communism that helped make this country the most dependable friend of anti-Communism; and helped make possible and fruitful also the noble Polish fidelity to Christianity that eventually began the overthrow of Communism with the election of a Polish pope. I personally witnessed the commencement of the de-stabilization of European Communism in a two-week visit to Poland in 1979 that happened to coincide with the Polish Pope's first return home.

But the effects in our country of eight decades of anti-historical and anti-metaphysical schooling, due largely to that dominance of Dewey-Kilpatrick "Progressivism" that Kandel deplored, have badly weakened our national mind and memory and the Western tradition to which our wisest intellectual compatriots, from the Founding Fathers and Federalists onwards, have always felt loyalty. Given the skepticism about the basic propositions of our founding ideas, documents, and institutions evinced by influential historians such as Charles Beard and Carl Becker, it was left to the Catholic John Courtney Murray to give a convincing rational defense of "the American Proposition" in *We Hold These Truths* in 1960. In addition, the great Jewish Natural Law school that descends remotely from Leo Strauss, and is found most influentially in Harry V. Jaffa and his students and in the works of David Novak, provides a kind of profound vindication of the wisdom and generosity of George Washington's welcoming letter to the Touro Synagogue in Newport, Rhode Island, on the subject of American citizenship.

Partly due to the "Progressive" educational experimentation of the "cult of uncertainty" in our schooling, an ignorant and arrogant nihilism has increasingly characterized American commercial, cultural, political, and intellectual life. Richard John Neuhaus has memorably described the denuding of our public life of a coherent transcendental-moral framework whereby we could with some confidence live and die by the proposition of self-evident truths in a God-directed world. Alasdair MacIntyre has followed C.S. Lewis in a far ampler, more scholarly way in describing a world "after virtue," and the invaluable

Gertrude Himmelfarb has described "the de-moralization of society," whereby traditional, rationally-intelligible virtues have been converted into subjective, arbitrary "values" impervious to rational criticism. The "abolition of man" means the evisceration of any normative, unitary idea of "civilization," and the elevation of a militant but very selective agenda of "tolerance" in its place (Ogden Nash!). We no longer have a civilization, we only have anthropological "cultures," none of any ultimate or authoritative worth. I appreciate Hugh Trevor-Roper's phrase for our ersatz secular morality: he called it the reign of "political correctitude." Rather nice, that: falsely pretending to be able to prescind from ethics, political correctness assumes the mantle of rectitude! "political correctitude"!

From the standpoint of tertiary education and our teaching corps, the Dewey/Kilpatrick victory in the lower schools is now fully consolidated in the world of teachers' colleges and education schools. However generous their fluctuating intentions, the victorious "Progressives" have done their damage in destroying the teaching of history, in favor of social-studies "political correctitude"; and in failing adequately to convey a basic curriculum in the K-8 grades that would enable our young people to build knowledge and skill within a coherent, sequenced, cumulative course of studies—such as every other developed country in the world now has and uses more effectively, and less expensively, than we do (4). In this regard, if we want to salvage the University for the future renaissance that we need, it behooves us to pay close attention to the courageous renewal of K-8 public education that has been undertaken in this country, with very limited means and against great odds and opposition, by E.D. Hirsch and his Core Knowledge Foundation.

In addition to the monolithic teachers' colleges, the tenure system in the colleges and universities presents us with a profound problem. Established and self-replicating radical cultural and left-utilitarian political ideas have been combined with a radically nominalist approach to scholarship in the Humanities and Social Sciences that valorizes the novel, odd, strange, violent, perverse, counter-intuitive, and anti-traditional. "The cult of uncertainty" valorizes brilliant "neophilia," the love of the "new approach" at all costs. "Everything is at sea but the fleet." We hold no truths to be self-evident. As Jacques Barzun noted almost a half-century ago, the triumph of scientific prestige and power in the post-Darwinian university was not so much an attack on literature and the arts as it was an attack on and demotion of the classical languages—the bearers of tradition—and on logic and mathematics. The winners argued, Barzun wrote, "that the study of these four subjects overtrained memory and the deductive faculties." (5) Looking back on the victorious "Progressive" professoriat from the historical vantage point of 1946, Aldous Huxley wrote ironically, "let us build a pantheon to professors," and suggested situating it in one of the bomb-gutted cities of Europe or Asia.

If we think of the powerful memory and deductive reasoning abilities that our greatest statesman, Abraham Lincoln, developed from sparse literary resources that included the Bible, Shakespeare, and Blackstone's Commentaries, but also Euclid, we may be reminded of what can happen to a culture that makes vast expenditures on education, but whose graduates increasingly know little logic and mathematics and only enough history to have contempt for it.

A long line of distinguished thinkers, including modern Catholic thinkers such as the Italian Don Luigi Sturzo, Paul Johnson, and the Hungarian-American Stanley Jaki, have reminded us that history and philosophy are only separable from one another for academic purposes: "To write history is to do philosophy," as Jaki recently put it.(6) A decade-by-decade narrative history of the twentieth century (or any century) inevitably entails and imposes ethics on the writer or reader, the teacher or student or citizen. There is no history without the evaluation of conduct. Lincoln refused to let Douglas prescind from the ethical question of slavery in Illinois in 1858. Lewis's *Abolition of Man* is partly a critique of half-witted "Progressive" school textbooks that pervasively debunked ethics as non-cognitive, sentimental, superstitious, and arbitrary. Kandel reproached the Dewey/Kilpatrick "Progressives" for the feckless, experimental "cult of uncertainty" that they indulged in the lower schools, with inevitable and dismal effect on general culture and higher education.

E.D. Hirsch has carefully and plausibly argued for the importance of actual historical and biographical narratives in both history/social sciences and literature/language arts in the elementary-school curriculum. At the college level, Columbia, the University of Chicago, the St. John's Colleges, some Evangelical and many Catholic colleges—some of them small, renegade institutions—have nobly opposed the virtual assassination of memory, Aristotelian common sense, and the humane patrimony of the West. Yet our feckless intellectual masters have indulged a long love affair with post-modern relativism and promiscuous paradox instead.

The catholic authority of reason was academically initiated by Socrates, Plato, and Aristotle, and was conveyed through Greco-Roman culture to St. John, St. Paul, and the Church. We believe in a "rational service" (Romans 12:1-2) that implicitly affirms the divinity of reason, of the Logos, the classic view for which C.S. Lewis argued in 1943, and which the pope reaffirmed at Regensburg in protesting the "de-Hellenization" of the Christian religion. More recently, this philosophical pope has again deftly and movingly identified the crucial matrix of our historical moment, in which philosophy and history are separable only for academic purposes, but not within the human person or the human commonwealth: the "attitude of resignation with regard to truth," he said in Austria earlier this month, "lies at the heart of the crisis of the West," for "if truth does not exist for man, then neither can he ultimately distinguish between good and evil." (7)

The orthodox tradition of moral reasoning is based on what Matthew Arnold called "the old but true Socratic thesis of the interdependence of virtue and knowledge" (8). Students who reach college able to read well and knowing some history—even if only the catastrophic history of the 20th century—are implicitly disposed to this tradition. A decent curriculum will introduce it to them—if no longer in Socrates, Plato, and Aristotle, let us hope at least in American history or in the works of Shakespeare, Milton, Johnson, Burke, the Federalists, Jane Austen, Newman, C.S. Lewis, T.S. Eliot, et al. "We cannot make truth," Samuel Johnson wrote, "it is our business only to find it." (9)

But in addition to history and literature and philosophy, logic and mathematics, whose modern demotion Barzun has noted, are also crucial for a reason other than themselves. They are the necessary preconditions to apprehend the natural sciences, which are a crucial test for the catholicity of reason in the modern university. Here, as in the case of Newman, it seems to me that the Catholic tradition has generated a witness of remarkable value for the contemporary university. Almost thirty years ago, I stumbled on a book by the physicist and historian and philosopher of science, Fr. Stanley L. Jaki, that went a long way toward solving, to my own satisfaction at least, some problems that had increasingly bothered me, and about which I will only say that they concerned the relations in my own mind and in reality between three large blocks of knowledge that to some degree I possessed, but whose relationships were obscure to me. I was not alone: the logic of the modern "multiversity" is centrifugal and nominalist, and as even Noam Chomsky has recently argued, the unification of the sciences on the positivist paradigm is today only wishful thinking. (10) Jaki's work is, by contrast, a detailed, sustained, polymathic rational testimony to the intelligibility of the true and the good, "of the interdependence of virtue and knowledge." Wider knowledge of it in the contemporary university—including the Catholic university— would be a great good. (11)

In conclusion, I would like to pay tribute to this heroic life of scholarship and intellectual integration and synthesis. Stanley L. Jaki's vast, wide-ranging, and lucid body of work seems to me one of the most impressive intellectual feats of recent times. It bears witness to the catholicity of reason, to the promise and possibility of the modern university honestly open to the true and the good, and to the capacity of disciplined individual scholars in the light of the Catholic tradition to redeem the time and serve as perhaps a saving remnant of intellectual life from which renewal and even renaissance can come. If the word "prophetic" was apt for 19th-century intellectuals such as Kierkegaard, Newman, Burckhardt, Leo XIII, and for their successors such as T.S. Eliot, C.S. Lewis, Gilson, Maritain, and the last two great popes, it is also apt for the profound, lucid, though sometimes combative and acidulous Father Stanley Jaki, a source of renewal for the contemporary mind and the contemporary university. He is not at ease in Babylon, nor should the rest of us be.

Dr. Michael D. Aeschliman is the author of *The Restitution of Man: C.S. Lewis and the Case against Scientism* (1983, 1998). He has written widely for such journals as *National Review* and *First Things.* He has taught at Columbia University, the University of Virginia, the Université Populaire de Lausanne (Switzerland), the Catholic University of Milan (Italy), and the

University of Italian Switzerland. Since 1971 he has been associated with the American School in Switzerland (TASIS) and with its affiliated schools and programs. He is the founder and director of the Erasmus Institute, and, since 1996, he has run the annual Erasmus-Jefferson Summer Institute in Tuscany (Italy) in collaboration with the Jefferson Scholars Program of the University of Virginia. Dr. Aeschliman has long-standing interests in international education, the philosophy of education, religion and education, literature and science, literature, as well as in literature, art, and ethics.

Endnotes

[1]On Kandel, see Diane Ravitch, *Left Back: A Century of Failed School Reforms* (NY, 2000), pp.314-321.

[2]Richard Weikart, *From Darwin to Hitler* (NY, 2004)

[3]NY, 1995.

[4]E.D. Hirsch, *The Schools We Need and Why We Don't Have Them* (NY, 1996); *The Knowledge Deficit* (Boston, 2006). I reviewed the latter in *The Weekly Standard*, 29 January 2007. For an earlier appreciation of Hirsch's project, see my "Culture and Anarchy," in *The World and I* (Washington), February 1988.

[5]Jacques Barzun, *Science: The Glorious Entertainment* (NY, 1964), p.147.

[6]S.L. Jaki, *Means to Message* (Grand Rapids, Michigan, 1999), p.199.

[7]*New York Times*, 9 September 2007, 11.

[8]Arnold, 1877, in *Essays Religious and Mixed, ed. R.H. Super* (Ann Arbor, Michigan, 1972), 162. See also Charles Larmore, "Beyond Naturalism," in *The Morals of Modernity* (Cambridge, 1996), esp. pp.102, 116-117; and R.E. Allen's Introduction to his new translation of *Plato's Republic* (New Haven, 2006).

[9]Sermon quoted in The Cambridge Companion to Samuel Johnson, ed. G. Clingham (Cambridge, 1997), p.207. For a careful, capacious, and thoughtful treatment of Johnson's orthodox epistemology and ethics, see Scott D. Evans, *Samuel Johnson's "General Nature"* (Newark, Delaware, 1999). For Shakespeare's unique importance to the English-speaking peoples as a moral teacher see my own "Why Shakespeare Was Not a Relativist and Why It Matters Now," *The Journal of Education* (Boston), Vol. 180, No.3 (1998), pp.51-66.

[10]Noam Chomsky, *On Nature and Language*, ed. A. Belletti and L. Rizzi (Cambridge, 2002), ch. 2-3. Very valuable essays.

[11]Several of my own reviews of Jaki's work over the last 25 years were re-printed in the *Vatican Secretariat for Scientific Studies Bulletin* (Oxford/Nijmegen/Rome), No.66 (October 2006).

SESSION V

Catholic Education at Non-Catholic Institutions

Radiating Jesus in Word and Sacrament: The Role of Catholic Campus Ministry at a Non-Catholic University[1]

Reverend Monsignor Stuart W. Swetland

It can not be stated too often or too clearly. We have the duty to share the faith, to evangelize and to teach. This is the command of our Lord and Savior, Jesus Christ, as he prepared to ascend to the Father:

> Then Jesus approached and said to them, "All power in heaven and on earth has been given to me. Go, therefore, and make disciples of all nations, baptizing them in the name of the Father, and of the Son, and of the holy Spirit, teaching them to observe all that I have commanded you. And behold, I am with you always, until the end of the age."[2]

This evangelization and teaching must flow from our own experience of the power of the Risen Lord. We hand on what we have received (cf. 1 Cor. 15:1ff) from our own personal relationship with the Lord in the community of his Church. We share with others what we have heard and seen:

> What was from the beginning, what we have heard, what we have seen with our eyes, what we looked upon and

> touched with our hands concerns the Word of life—for the life was made visible; we have seen it and testify to it and proclaim to you the eternal life that was with the Father and was made visible to us—what we have seen and heard we proclaim now to you, so that you too may have fellowship with us; for our fellowship is with the Father and with his Son, Jesus Christ. We are writing this so that our joy may be complete.[3]

Our joy is made complete in sharing what we have received.

Between 80-85% of college bound Catholics decide to attend non-Catholic universities and colleges. Since it is well documented that the most vital years of a person's journey in faith are the ages 18-25, it is incumbent on the Church to focus its resources and pastoral energy on these young people.[4]

What is at the Center?

Historians often cite the axiom that you can tell what a particular culture or era values most by what they place at the center of their cities, towns, or villages. In the middle ages, an age of faith, the cathedral or church dominated city center. By the nineteenth century, town halls or seats of governments were more the focus of attention. The twentieth century saw the shift towards shopping as first Main Street and then the shopping center or mall became the central focus of activity.

By the end of the twentieth century and into the twenty-first, there has been a noticeable shift. Social commentaries now recognize that with our current urban sprawl and dislocation there is in fact no real center of gravity to our towns and cities. Many see this as a reflection of out post-modern culture. They say that post-modernism's emphasis on relativism and a hermeneutics of suspicion about any system, truth claim, or ideology tends towards a constant de-centering.

Ministering to modern college students must take this cultural reality into consideration. One must try to reach young adults where they are and not where on might wish them to be. Fortunately, someone did this for me. I am Catholic today because of Newman Ministry.

I am a product of Newman Ministry. I became Catholic at the Newman Center of Oxford University while a Rhodes Scholar in the early 1980s. A typical member of the Baby Boom generation, the

Campus Ministry attracted me by its willingness to deal with my search for "personal fulfillment." By the time I was ordained and assigned as a priest to Newman work at Bradley University in the early 1990s, a whole new generation, Generation X, was going to university. Although the basic ministerial needs had not changed, Generation X's approach to life was very different from the Boomers.

Today a new generation populates our campuses. At St. John's Catholic Newman Center at the University of Illinois (where I worked for almost a decade), we housed more than 300 students each year and we saw several thousand more attend Mass and participate in our programs and classes. All the campus ministers on my staff and I agreed that Generation Y is definitely not like Generation X.

Birth Date	Nickname	Church
1920-1939	Greatest Generation	Pre-Vatican II
1940-1960	Baby Boomers	Vatican II
1960-1979	Gen X	Post Vatican II
1980 –	Millennial/Gen Y	"New Faithful"

The Millennials

Because of my experience with Catholic campus ministry, I am often asked how best to minister to young adults today. This is an important question to answer. Generation Y or the Millennials are the first truly post-modern generation. This generation, born after 1980, has grown up with computers and cable, AIDS and America Online, Challenger and Columbine, 9/11 and the war on terror. They do not know or remember President Reagan, the Cold War, the first Gulf War, or an Italian Pope. South Africa and Russia have always been democratic. School and work have always been a potentially dangerous place to be.

Many expect that a generation born and raised in an era of post-modern relativism would reflect this philosophy. Yet, the Millennial generation has caught many by surprise, especially in its thirst for religion and spirituality. This is particularly true of college administrators. Sadly, it has also caught some in church leadership by surprise too. Just when it is needed the most, many dioceses and religious orders are scaling back their commitments to ministry in higher education.

Let there be no doubt. The Millennials are searching for spiritual, religious, and moral truth. Numerous studies have borne this out including the recently issued report by the Higher Education Research Institute of UCLA, *Spirituality in Higher Education: A National Study of College Students' Search for Meaning and Purpose* (www.spirituality.ucla.edu). The summary statement of this study of 46 colleges and universities states:

> Results showed that students have deeply felt spiritual and religious values, are very much engaged in spiritual and religious pursuits, and that such pursuits are far more important to them than most people may assume. But there are clear indications that institutions are not encouraging students to delve into these issues, and academic and campus programs do not seem to support these interests.

Our Catholic campus ministry must provide this much-needed support.

While it is always problematic to generalize about such a large group of people (80 million—twice as large as Generation X), it is particularly difficult to do so about this generation. They have no one hairstyle or clothing preference. Whatever may be true of the majority, there is a large and often vocal minority that is exactly the opposite. For example, while it is true that Generation Y is, on the whole, spiritually searching, the UCLA study shows that there is a significant minority that is indifferent about whether or not there is a Supreme Being. Any experienced campus minister knows that generational generalities never do full justice to the unique and diverse reality of those we are privileged to serve.

This being said, there are some general trends that do help to describe the majority of the Millennials, especially those who choose to attend college or university. For example, they are the "organizational kids," called by David Brooks the "future workaholics of America." Their whole lives have been planned, scheduled, and structured. Even playtime was structured and supervised for them, and their so-called free time was full of scheduled activity for "enrichment." In college they continue this trend, attempting to do everything and build a "killer C.V."

In my experience, they are goal-oriented and dominated by an achievement ethos. This makes them very accepting of the established order and deferential to those in authority. They would rather "surf" through and around the structures and "powers that be" than fight the machine. They are earnest and follow the rules.

They are also very optimistic and cheerful. This is true even though they grew up in a very safety-conscious world where any place was potentially dangerous. They were born when children had become the focus of the home, and most of them get along with their parents (90%) and basically share their parents' values (75%) (cf. Howe and Strauss, *Millennials Rising*).

They like to study and socialize in groups. Friends are of the utmost importance. They are generous, open, and tolerant perhaps to a fault. They have little time for "big issues," are often indifferent to politics, and are most likely to identify themselves as political independents. They usually spend about eight hours a day in front of either a T.V. or a computer screen. They are not great readers, but are immersed in other forms of media. While spiritually hungry, most Millennials are broadly uncatechized in their religious tradition no matter what tradition that may be.

Professor Mary Ann Glendon of Harvard University, recently named American Ambassador to the Holy See, speaks about today's university students in the terms of "bright spots" and "shadows."[5] To Ambassador Glendon, this generation is blessed in many ways. They are the most privileged ever in reference to education, especially for women. More of them knew and grew up with their grandparents alive than past generations. They and the computer grew-up together making most of them very "tech-savvy."[6]

But there are also many shadows in the lives of the Millennials. There was abortion on demand, meaning that approximately one-third of them did not make it out of the womb. Although the social science has yet to fully demonstrate this fact, I believe this has had a subtle psychological and spiritual effect on Gen Y. Many of them suffer from an insecurity where they feel the need to constantly prove that they were worthy of being "chosen to live." They have lived in the shadow of AIDS, dealt with the breakdown of many of their or their friends' families, and have had an almost universally poor religious formation. Most centrally, many of them grew-up in a world where their boomer parents were focused on "personal fulfillment" rather than raising children. The result has been a general loss of trust and hope and an inability to defend our beliefs even to ourselves.[7]

But despite the shadows, Glendon sees that above all the Millennials are a generation in search of meaning:

> What emerges from these data and impressions, it seems to me, is a portrait of a generation that is searching—a generation of young men and women who want something better for themselves and their future children than what was handed on to them; a generation that is exploring uncharted territory and finding little guidance from its elders...To sum up, then: I would suggest that the "Y" in Generation Y might stand for yearning—yearning, questioning, searching, refusing to be satisfied with easy answers.

Campus Ministry must be there to assist this generation in their quest for meaning. Very recent polls and studies have confirmed Glendon's main point. Gen Y is not indifferent or closed to religion. In fact they are very open to hearing and experiencing faith. In a poll conducted by the Associated Press and MTV in April of 2007, only 14% of 1280 young people (ages 13-24) said that "religion and spirituality doesn't play a role in their lives; while 44% said that spirituality and religion was "very important" and a further 21% said that it was "somewhat important." Twenty percent said that religion played a "small part" in their lives.[8] Interestingly the AP/MTV poll also showed that those involved in religion were significantly more likely to self-identify as happy than those who were not interested.

These poll numbers are similar to the results of a major study done at the University of North Carolina.[9] This study showed a "strong religious component" for approximately two-thirds of young people. Those that identify with religion also practice their faith at a high rate. For example, almost two-thirds of American young people pray daily or weekly. In addition, despite various scandals in the Protestant Community and the Catholic Church, the approval rate for religious organizations remains very high with only 20% rating them "poor" or "very poor."

This means that most young people want a real relationship with God. On a whole, the majority are hungry for spiritual fulfillment. Granted there is a stubborn 15-35% that are not as open to faith, but they are a minority. We ought to be searching for ways to reach this group as well, but the good news is that the "bad news" that you often hear about the current generation is not true.

Ministering to the Millennials

How does one minister to such a generation? First, we must be present to them, ministering to them in authentic relationships. Between the ages of 18-25, most young people of any generation make momentous decisions that will shape their lives. They will go from an inherited faith (or no faith) to one they "own" as their own. They will choose their vocation in life. They will solidify or make many of the most significant relationships of their lives. We best serve by accompanying them on this pilgrimage.

Second, we must provide answers to their questions. The most effective way to do this is by offering our own witness and by helping our students discover the answers themselves.

Any experienced campus minister knows that you can't talk down to Generation Y. The Millennials like to draw their own conclusions, and they want us to be authentic in our answers. They don't want us to try to be what we aren't; they want us to stay true to what advertisers call "brand DNA." They want straight talk with utter confidence and total accountability. Campus ministers are not teenagers, and we ought not try to pretend we are. They want us, faithfully, frankly, and fully, to represent the teaching of the Church. They will hear dissent and attacks from other quarters.They expect (and, in justice, deserve) authentic Catholic teaching, whole and entire from us.

Liturgically, they are a mixed bag. I believe here, as in other areas, we must follow St. Paul's admonition "to become all things to all that I may be all means save some" (1 Cor. 9:22b). Contemporary services, traditional worship, and devotions of all types find niche groups of dedicated followers. I do find that Generation Y tends to prefer their religious practices to be highly "incarnational." Statues and icons, "bells and smells," rosaries and chaplets—all of these things are tangible and "real" to young people who spend so much of their time in virtual reality.

But above all, the Millennials are a generation searching for community. Nearly all young adults of any generation at some point perceive themselves to be lonely. But this perception is particularly acute for the Millennials. Whether this feeling is real or just perceived is arguable. Nevertheless, it seems true to them. To many Generation Y college students, loneliness is a key issue, especially those who seek out campus ministers and ministry. They have grown up lonely. They are starved for love and affection. They are a generation that has grown up with few siblings and without a close extended family. Many of them are from broken homes. Usually both parents worked outside the home, and sometimes their careers came first. This means that emotionally, many Millennials perceive themselves consciously or unconsciously to be, as John Paul II has called them, "orphans of living parents."

They are looking for true communion—a communion centered on a real, personal relationship with the God who has revealed Himself in Jesus. They are attracted to the fact that the Lord understands and shares in their suffering—the emptiness and loneliness and abandonment that so many of them feel. But they do not wish to dwell only on the pain. The *Passion* may have its place, but they want to experience the power of the Resurrected Lord. They long—as we all do—for the peace, joy, and communion made possible in Jesus.

This longing means that our campus ministry must be Christocentric and provide a place for true fellowship. We must provide spaces, places, and opportunities for prayer and communion. Of particular help is the formation of small group fellowships of various sorts. These Bible studies, prayer circles, and service groups can act as a "mediating structure" between the often large and intimidating realities of university and Church and the lonely individual. We must aid their search for answers and be "always ready to give a reason for our hope" (1 Pt. 3:15). They will then allow us to lead them towards service and discovery of their vocation in Christ.

Campus ministry is obviously a daunting task. It is only possible if we radiate Jesus Christ in all things. Especially, we must radiate Him in Word and Sacrament. As Hans Urs von Balthasar wrote at the end of his life: "For this reason, lest everything in the Church become superficial and insipid, the true, undiminished program for the Church today must read: the greatest possible radiance in the world by virtue of the closest possible following of Christ."[10] This quotation is reflected in the mission statement of St. John's Catholic Newman Center:

> The St. John's Catholic Newman Center exists to radiate Jesus Christ in all things by encouraging those who live, worship, and work within this community to serve others and to strive toward the highest ideals of Christian spiritual,

> moral, and intellectual development as lived and taught in
> the rich tradition of the Catholic Church.

Thus I believe that our work of accompaniment with the Millennial Generation is best fulfilled when our own struggle to be good disciples allows us to radiate the joy and pace of walking with the Lord.

Many commentators have noticed a decline in religious education of both Generation X and Y. These studies need not be cited here again. Anyone who has worked with young adults over the last forty years will attest to this fact. Forty years is two biblical generations. The situation is that now the current generations of college students are the sons and daughters of a generation that was itself poorly catechized. Many parents, confronted with the awesome task of educating their children in the faith, have discovered just how much they themselves do not know. Nancy Yos commented on this situation in a highly provocative article in *First Things*:

> No, the situation could hardly be more serious, unless Diocletian reclined still in his palace, and martyrs still faced night arrest and torture in the amphitheaters. The situation could hardly be more dire, unless the old Roman law still survived that stated flatly, frighteningly, "It is unlawful for Christians to exist." No such law operates today, but the Catholic Church in the United States behaves as if one did. The situation is this: that the Catholic Church in the United States is committing suicide through refusal to educate its people…We do not know even the fundamentals of our religion, and we are not stupid. If the fundamentals had ever been given to us, I think we could have absorbed them…But they were not given….No teacher ever stood up in any classroom of mine and made any positive statement beginning with the words, "This is so."…Surely the American Church could have hinted at the weightiness of the faith, even to children, even to us. We might have learned how old this faith is, how heavy in history, how complex in tradition and deadly serious in creed….To this pass: that the most privileged Catholics who have ever lived should be taught by their Church that their religion is a lie; for being kept purposely ignorant of it is the same thing as being told it is a lie…"I saved the Cross," says Chesterton's Father Brown, "as the Cross will always be saved." I wish it were so, but I am afraid. Maybe not for us. Not here.[11]

Fr. Alfred McBride, O. Praem., speaks of the "religious illiteracy" that has ensued:

> Here I wish to draw your attention to the matter of what some call a religious "illiteracy" among our young Catholics... Frankly, they are not learning the [religious code] words, let alone the content and meaning of the terms...Such competence ought to be the sign of a trained, informed, and literate Catholic...As for doctrine, students still think that the Immaculate Conception is the Virgin Birth. Grace remains a mystery for them even as an identifiable term. Sad to say they have neither a pre- nor a post-Vatican II appreciation of miracles and find the resurrection of the dead as puzzling as an obscure term found in the *New York Times* Sunday crossword puzzle. They have yet to find a way of decoding eternal life and the significance of faith as a gift. I would never claim that such lofty doctrines ought to be grasped in depth by young students. It is not a question of depth perception so much as any perception at all. The great Christian doctrines will always keep us in awe and silence before the mystery. But we need to know what to be in awe about.[12]

No one ought to be complacent in light of this situation. We who have been privileged, graced, and blessed to be given the faith have the moral duty to share it with others. It is, after all, the greatest gift we can give, for at the heart and center of it all, we are introducing others to Him whom we love.

Another reason that we, as a fellowship and as educators, ought to be quite concerned with the widespread reality of religious illiteracy is that nature hates a vacuum. Something will rush in to fill the vacuum left by the lack of authentic education in the faith. And in America, that something often is a vague form of "content-light" faith called by Christian Smith and Melinda Lundquist Denton "moralistic therapeutic deism."[13]

Smith and Denton's analysis flows from their work at University of North Carolina on the data gathered by the National Study of Youth and Religion cited above. While the current generation continues the tradition American openness to religion and the spiritual life, Smith and Denton noticed a striking similarity among the millennial generation about basic beliefs even across denominational and creedal lines. Their tentative conjecture was summarized as follows:

We advance our thesis somewhat tentatively as less than a conclusive fact but more than conjecture: we suggest that the *de facto* dominant religion among contemporary U.S. teenagers is what we might call "Moralistic Therapeutic Deism." The creed of this religion, as codified from what emerged from our interviews, sounds something like this:
1. A God exists who created and orders the world and watches over human life on earth.
2. God wants people to be good, nice, and fair to each other, as taught in the Bible and by most world religions.
3. The central goal in life is to be happy and to feel good about oneself.
4. God does not need to be particularly involved in one's life except when God is needed to resolve a problem.
5. Good people go to heaven when they die.[14]

This is the creed of many young "believers" across denominational lines. It is a far cry from the faith of orthodox Christianity. However, it is the default position that many Americans have traditionally fallen into. Some commentators have referred to this as the "Americanization" of religion. It is remarkably similar to the findings of Will Herberg back in the middle of the twentieth century and that Barry Kosmin and Seymour Lachman verified in the 1990's.[15] These studies showed that the majority of self-professed believers in America are more likely to have their beliefs "Americanized" by the cultural system of the United States then they are to attempt to allow their religion to influence the American system. These studies should be examined.[16]

The first study is the famous essay in religious sociology published by Herberg in 1955. Herberg's book, *Protestant-Catholic-Jew*, was dedicated to the "third generation," meaning by this, the third generation after immigration to America. These were the grandsons and granddaughters of immigrants. Herberg noticed a general "return" of this generation to the religious practices of their ancestors, rejecting their parents' rejection of religion. But he also noted that despite this religious revival, the "trend towards secularism"[17] in ideas, beliefs and practices had not been abated. In fact, despite their religious difference, Americans seemed to profess a certain uniformity of belief that Herberg calls "The American Way of Life":

It seems to me that a realistic appraisal of the values, ideas and behavior of the American people leads to the conclusion that Americans, by and large, do have their "common religion" and that "that religion" is the system familiarly known as the American Way of Life. It is the American Way of Life that supplies American society with an "overarching sense of unity" and conflict. It is the American Way of Life about which Americans are admittedly and unashamedly "intolerant." It is the American Way of Life that provides the framework in terms of which the crucial values of American existence are couched. By every realistic criterion the American Way of Life is the objective faith of the American people.[18]

Herberg describes this American Way of Life as individualistic, dynamic, pragmatic, humanitarian, generous, and optimistic.[19] Its spirituality is a "certain kind of idealism," and "it stresses incessant activity."[20] It has a belief in progress education and self-improvement.[21] Herberg believes that it is best characterized by the word "democracy." In words strikingly similar to Michael Novak's description of democratic capitalism,[22] Herberg explains:

If the American Way of Life had to be defined in one word, "democracy" would undoubtedly be the word, but democracy in a peculiarly American sense. On its political side it means the Constitution; on its economic side, an equalitarianism which is not only compatible with but indeed actually implies vigorous economic competition and high mobility.[23]

Herberg summarizes his argument by stating emphatically that the "secularization of religion could hardly go further."[24] Herberg was writing in 1955 about the paradox of great numbers of religious adherents whose actual religion had "lost much of its authentic Christian (or Jewish) content."[25] Barry Kosmin and Seymour P. Lachman return to this paradox in their study of American religion, *One Nation Under God.* Their work is an analysis of the results of a 1990 survey of 113,000 people across the continental United States called the National Survey of Religious Identification" (NSRI).[26] Kosmin and Lachman's study shows that Herberg's main thesis is still valid for America. They write, "While America may be among the most religiously diverse nations, one can observe a process of Americanization at work on all its religions."[27] In Kosmin and Lachman's opinion this trend is most "vividly portrayed" among American Catholics who were closer in many beliefs to their fellow citizens than they were to their bishops.[28] They point to an underlying syncretism at work in America. This process means that the "minority religions" become Protestantized and the Protestant churches become Americanized. In addition, there is in American society a powerful civil religion at work.[29] They write:

> A corollary problem of contemporary American society is that despite his or her more frequent church attendance, the thoughts and values of the average churchgoer are less often derived from religious sources than from secular ones. Gerhard Lanski wrote that this is an example of a "transcendental faith. . .gradually being transformed into a cultural faith." A generation ago this was truer of Protestants than of members of other faiths, but Catholics and Jews are now moving in this direction, too. What is there in American history and the American environment that propels this movement?

Kosmin and Lachman cannot fully answer this vital question by statistical methods or sociology. However, in their conclusion, they attempt to venture an opinion. They believe that in the United States, secularism and religion each use and are reinforced by the other:

> In other nations, in countries as different as Italy and Algeria, the tension between religion and secularism is more pronounced than it is in the United States, where secularism and religion regularly use and redefine each other. Religion in the United States frequently sanctifies the goals of a basically secular society, and the secular society affects and influences the very meaning of religious identification and association. It is therefore not surprising that America appears to be growing more secular precisely at a time when religious identification is highly pronounced.[30]

The best example of this mutual reinforcement, Kosmin and Lachman argue, is the American understanding of religious liberty. Americans have a tendency to believe that religious liberty applies not just to the state ("Congress shall make no laws ....") but also to one's own relationship with one's own religious organization. For example, eight out of ten Americans believe that their religious beliefs should be decided independent of organized religion.[31] They write, "Our democratic society breeds the notion that if all creeds can co-exist, then they must be fundamentally similar."[32]

Kosmin and Lachman notice that there is in modern America society a backlash against the trend towards secularization among some religious groups—most noticeably among the so-called "fundamentalist." Even in the more mainline denominations there exists among a significant minority a desire for more traditional values and religious practices. But even this traditionalist movement is up against very powerful "countervailing trends" that are undermining it. These trends, according to Kosmin and Lachman, are mainly economic in origin. Economic pressures require great mobility that undermine community life and break down close-knit extended families. Economic necessity requires most families to have two wage earners, taking mothers away from their traditional role as primary care-giver to their children. Competition in the marketplace ensures an ever-expanding search for innovation, new ways, and new consumer goods. These goods and services must be marketed, which usually means being sold by advertising that further undermines family values and stability.[33] Kosmin and Lachman note:

> These opposing forces create the paradoxical nature of American religion, to which we have often referred. There appears to be a collective schizophrenia whereby the public says one thing, with apparent sincerity, in answer to public-opinion polls and acts quite differently. The modern and the traditional become both seductive and repulsive simultaneously. America's market-oriented religion bears a similarity to the rest of society in its hopeful and optimistic tone and its unwillingness to face certain uncomfortable realities.[34]

They conclude their study by stating that the trends that they noted show no signs of abating in the near future. In fact, they believe that the "Protestantization of American Society" will most likely accelerate as the general pace of society accelerates.[35]

These sociological studies indicate that there might be an "inner logic" at work in at least the American incarnation of democratic capitalism. But these studies are only descriptive. They can and have raised serious questions that must be addressed, but sociology cannot give the answers. Most importantly, the question raised by Kosmin and Lachman should be discussed: What is there in American history and the American environment that propels the secularization (in the way described above) of a self-professedly religious people?

First there could be an argument over facts. Perhaps these studies somehow missed the mark. Americans might not be dominated by the American Way of Life as described by Herberg or be so much at odds with their religious affiliation as Kosmin and Lachman argue. However, most people would not dispute the main results reported above. What might be disputed though is the course of this uniquely American style of secularization.

In his early writings, Michael Novak argued forcibly that American society did enforce a particular "standpoint" on its citizens. Novak taught that there were powerful cultural myths at work in American society. These myths included the myth of "the lonely individual" and of the "marketplace" but especially the "myth of the head (mind, rationality, impersonal logic)."[36] Novak calls this dominant myth a "Nordic, Anglo-Saxon consciousness":

> The image that has controlled the development of American culture is that of the "melting pot." That image was always misleading, for, in fact, a Nordic, Anglo-Saxon consciousness dominated American life, a Protestant consciousness, setting the style for what might be experienced, intuited and decided. In order to prosper in the United States, possibly even to survive in the United States, immigrants from other ways of life had to pay a price. That price was the Americanization of their psyches. They had to cease being what they were, and to learn the ways of Nordic, Anglo-Saxon culture in its setting in the new world.[37]

This is an interesting description of the type of process discussed in Herberg's and Kosmin and Lachman's work. And it is consistent with the conjecture of Smith and Denton concerning "moralistic therapeutic deism."

The difficulty with this trend is that it makes effective evangelization nearly impossible. It is as if this "Americanized religion" is like an inoculation against the authentic thing. The weak strain of the virus makes the host nearly impervious to the real thing. And have no doubt about it, "moralistic therapeutic deism" is not compatible with any robust version of the Catholic faith. The essayist Rod Dreher of the *Dallas Morning News* makes this point when discussing Benedict XVI's teaching against relativism:

> It's wrong and dangerous, though, to expect a religious believer to affirm that all beliefs about God could be

equally true—which is what Benedict's critics really demand. To do so would be to empty religion of its deepest meaning—to turn it into something that's merely socially or personally useful. That's where American religion is headed, however. Several years ago, researchers with the University of North Carolina's National Study of Youth and Religion polled American teenagers and found that faith was important to them. But it's faith not in established religion but rather in what NYSR's social scientists termed "Moralistic Therapeutic Deism." "Whatever that relativist mush is, it has little to do with the God of Abraham, Isaac and Jacob, or any traditional religion. Researchers concluded that either American youths don't know their traditions' teaching, or don't much care. Strikingly, they found that many teenagers interviewed had never discussed theology with an adult. The theological content of our faiths is fast eroding because of the lazy indifference of older generations to whom the traditions were delivered.[38]

This is why it is so essential to engage our students at non-Catholic colleges and university with the truth that has been revealed in Jesus. They are hungering for authentic spirituality, for the truth of the faith, for theological discussions of depth and substance. We can and should provide places and opportunities for these encounters to happen. We should be encouraging young people to seek, to knock, to ask. Ultimately, the answers to the fundamental questions that people ask are important because people matter. These questions and their answers point to the longing that is to be found in every heart. We want to know who we are and why we are. Ultimately, the answer is Jesus Christ. Jesus reveals us to ourselves and makes our eternal vocation clear to us. In Jesus, we discover *eternal life*: "And this is eternal life, that they know thee the only true God, and Jesus Christ whom thou hast sent" (Jn. 17:3).

Reverend Monsignor Stuart W. Swetland was ordained a priest in 1991 for the diocese of Peoria, Illinois. He first received a B.S. in physics from the United States Naval Academy. Elected a Rhodes Scholar in 1981, he entered the Catholic Church while studying at Oxford University, from which he holds a B.A. and M.A. in politics, philosophy, and economics. He also has an M.Div. and M.A. from Mount Saint Mary's Seminary in Emmitsburg,

Maryland. His S.T.L. and S.T.D. are from the Pontifical Lateran University, and he has also studied at the John Paul II Institute for Studies on Marriage and the Family in Washington. He is currently the Director of Homiletics Pre-Theology at Mount St. Mary's, but was formerly director and chaplain at the Cardinal Newman Center at the University of Illinois. He is currently also serving as the executive secretary of the Fellowship of Catholic Scholars.

Endnotes

[1]This essay in an expansion and revision of "Searching for Answers Today," the foreword to *Questions College Students Ask,* Christine Pinheiro and Kenneth J. Howell, Ph.D. (Urbana-Champaign : The Institute of Catholic Thought, St. John's Catholic Newman Center, The University of Illinois, 2006). St. John's Catholic Newman Center of the University of Illinois generously sponsored this presentation. I wish to dedicate this essay to the outstanding men and women who "fight the good fight of faith" at the University of Illinois.

[2]Matthew 28:18-20.

[3]1 John 1:1-4.

[4]"Campus Ministry Has Positive, Lifelong Effect on Faith", *CARA Report* Vol. 8, No.2, Fall 2002

[5]Many Ann Glendon, "University Students Today: Portrait of a Generation Search," *Pontifical Council of the Laity, Eighth Youth Forum,* Rome, April 2004.

[6]*Ibid.*

[7]*Ibid.*

[8]Eric Gorski and Trevor Tompson, "Poll: God Vital to Young Americans" (www. USATODAY.com, 8/24/2007).

[9]Christian Smith, Robert Faris, Melinda Lundquist Denton, Mark Regnerus, *Mapping American Adolescent Subjective Religiosity and Attitudes of Alienation Toward Religion: A Research Report,* Sociology of Religion 2003, 64:1, 111-133.

[10]Hans Urs von Balthasar, *My Work in Retrospect* (San Francisco: Ignatius Press, 1993), 57-58.

[11]Nancy Yos, "Touch Me: A Catholic *Cri de Coeur*," First Things, April, 1992.

[12]Father Alfred McBride, O. Praem., "Less than 60%...or Everything You Didn't Want to Know about Their Answers," *NCEA Religious Education Forum Newsletter.* June 1978. For an analysis of this report see Monsignor Michael J. Wrenn, *Catechisms and Controversies* (San Francisco: Ignatius Press, 1991), 134-137.

[13]Christian Smith and Melinda Lundquist Denton, *Soul Searching: The Religious and Spiritual Lives of American Teenagers* (Oxford: Oxford University Press, 2005), 162-71.

[14]*Ibid.,*162-3.

[15]Will Herberg, *Protestant-Catholic-Jew: An Essay in American Religious Sociology* (Chicago: University of Chicago Press, 1983). Herberg's work was initially published

in 1955. Barry A. Kosmin and Seymour P. Lachman, *One Nation Under God* (New York: Harmony Books, 1993).

[16]For a more detailed examination of these issues see Stuart W. Swetland, *Towards a Civilization of Love?* (Ann Arbor: UMI Company, 1998)

[17]Herberg, 1.

[18]*Ibid.* 75.

[19]*Ibid.,* 78-79.

[20]*Ibid.*

[21]*Ibid.,* 79.

[22]Cf. Michael Novak, *The Spirit of Democratic Capitalism* (New York: Simon and Schuster, 1982).

[23]Herberg., 78.

[24]*Ibid.,* 83.

[25]*Ibid.,* 3.

[26]Kosmin and Lachman, 1.

[27]*Ibid.,* 10.

[28]*Ibid.*

[29]*Ibid.,* 11-12.

[30]*Ibid.,* 280.

[31]*Ibid.*

[32]*Ibid.,* 11.

[33]*Ibid.,* 282.

[34]*Ibid.*

[35]*Ibid.,* 283.

[36]Michael Novak, Politics: *Realism and Imagination* (New York: Herder and Herder, 1971), 87.

[37]I*bid.,* 84.

[38]Rod Dreher, "Which Religion is the Right Religion?" *Dallas Morning News,* July 26, 2007

[39]*Gaudium et spes,* 22.

Catholicism in the Secular University

Robert Louis Wilken

"Let your speech be ordered wholly/ By an intellectual love;/ Elucidate the carnal maze/ With clear light from above."[1]

In the late sixties when I taught at Fordham University in New York City, it was said that most students were sons and daughters of firemen, policemen, or sanitation workers. That is probably an exaggeration, but it carries a truth nonetheless. Few parents were themselves college graduates, and the young person was usually the first in the family to attend college. Though the State University of New York had an extensive system of public higher education, Catholic parents preferred to pay a steeper tuition to have their child attend a Catholic university than go to the City University of New York or to Queens College. What counted most was not curriculum, programs of study, or academic excellence but that the school was Catholic.

Today it is estimated that eighty to ninety percent of the Catholics students who go to college in the United States matriculate in non-Catholic institutions. What is more, most students who graduate from Catholic high schools choose non-Catholic colleges. Given the number of Catholics in the United States, that adds up to a lot of students. In many colleges and universities, Catholics comprise twenty to thirty percent of the student body—or more.

The most visible sign of Catholicism on American college campuses is attendance at Mass. Catholics, like Evangelicals, go to church and, on weekends, Sunday evening in particular, students can be seen making their way to the university parish, a Catholic center on or near the campus, or a local parish. On Ash Wednesday, Catholics are identified by the smudge of black ash on their foreheads.

But when it comes to the intellectual life of the university, the lamp of Catholic thought is hidden under a bushel. An occasional faculty member, or a group of students, will join in a protest against abortion, but in public discussion and debate, it is rare to find a Catholic professor addressing the issues in a distinctively Catholic way. The Catholic presence runs the gamut from having pizza or spaghetti at a Newman center to protests or community service, but seldom does it reach into the library or lecture hall. Piety is evident; Catholic intellect and learning are not.

On university campuses, Catholic faculty are largely invisible. They are seldom known to students, and though many are accomplished scholars in their academic disciplines, few have the formation in Catholic culture or history to serve as mentors to students. More often than not their Catholicism is a private and personal thing, an affair of piety and practice, divorced from the intellectual enterprise that is the business of the university.

The absence of intellectual leadership on the part of Catholic faculty deprives students of models of well-educated Catholic laymen and laywomen who by their life and conversation display a mature and seasoned faith. Seldom will students find guides among the faculty who can deepen their understanding of Catholicism—suggesting a book here, an article there—as their studies present challenges to what they learned as youngsters. Sadly, many Catholic students will go through four years of college to become reasonably well informed in some area of study, European history, American literature, international politics, biology, and so on, yet leave the university children spiritually.

In the decades leading up to Vatican Council II, Catholic culture was deeper and more encompassing than it is today, and educated Catholics had a sense of being part of a long and venerable intellectual tradition that was very much alive in mid-twentieth century America. During the years between 1920 and 1960 American Catholicism went through a literary revival, fueled in the main by European writers such as G.K. Chesterton, George Bernanos, Charles Peguy, Sigrid Undset, Graham Green, Evelyn Waugh, and others. But there were also major American figures such as Flannery O'Connor, Walker Percy, J.F. Powers, and Allen Tate, to mention several of the more notable. These writers as well as philosophers such as Jacques Maritain and Étienne Gilson and the historian Christopher Dawson kept alive a lively Catholic intellectual tradition that gave educated

Catholics an imaginative grasp of the Catholic faith and an eagerness to interpret Catholicism within the increasingly secular culture of the United States.

Much of the cohesion of Catholic thinking came from the renascence of Thomism. In the course of the 19th century, neo-scholasticism had become a self-conscious philosophical outlook and it was given its intellectual charter by Pope Leo XIII in his encyclical *Aeterni Patris*. The pope urged Catholics to "restore the golden wisdom of St. Thomas, and to spread it far and wide for the defense and beauty of the Catholic faith, for the good of society, and for the advantage of all the sciences." In the early decades of this century, the appropriation of the philosophy of St. Thomas sparked an intellectual revival among American Catholics that lasted till mid century. Thomism was versatile and accessible to different kinds of thinkers, and it offered Catholics a unified intellectual vision that embraced all areas of life, including the arts.

Flannery O'Connor, the Catholic novelist, had the custom of reading from Thomas's *Summa* twenty minutes each night before going to bed. In one of her letters she says that if her mother came into the room and said, "Turn off that light. It's late," she would lift her finger with a "broad beatific expression" and reply: "The light being eternal and limitless, cannot be turned off. Shut your eyes." O'Connor was guided in her reading of Thomas by Jacques Maritain, in particular his *Art and Scholasticism*, from which she had learned that "art is wholly concerned with the good of that which is made." Maritain and Gilson, both of whom taught in the United States, gave Thomism a commanding place in Catholic intellectual life.

The Thomistic revival reached its zenith in the 1950s. But as Philip Gleason, the historian of American Catholicism, shows in *Contending with Modernity*, "hardly had this climax been reached when a decline set in that was so sudden and so steep as to justify calling it a collapse."

The reasons were several. Not least was the difficulty of teaching a philosophical "system" to thousands of undergraduates. The growing influence of Catholic biblical scholarship in the wake of the encyclical *Divino Afflante Spiritu* introduced a strong bias against scholasticism into Catholic thought. And in the 1950s, as the *nouvelle theologie* made its way across the Atlantic, it brought a critique of scholasticism from another quarter. But at bottom, Gleason observes, the loss of cohesion in Catholic intellectual life had less to do with any particular challenge than a loss of conviction that Catholicism had a unifying intellectual vision to offer.

This failure of nerve still afflicts Catholic intellectual life and has been weakened further by widespread ignorance of the Catholic tradition among educated Catholics. With the burgeoning number of Catholics students and faculty attending private and secular colleges, Catholics increasingly resemble other university graduates in their moral and intellectual outlook. Though well trained in other areas, unfamiliarity with the Catholic tradition puts them in a position of vulnerability and weakness in matters of faith. They often lack the capacity to defend or express their beliefs—even to themselves—and are ill equipped to give an account of their moral convictions in our relativistic culture.

One small example: A few years ago at the University of Virginia, the Christian Faculty Forum, a small ecumenical group of Christian faculty, devoted a few sessions to Christian views of gay marriage. At one session a Catholic member of the group came into the meeting with a column on gay marriage written the day before by William Raspberry, a columnist for the Washington Post. Raspberry had said that he did not understand why there was so much fuss over gay marriage. The Catholic member of the faculty read some passages from Raspberry's column to us and observed that he thought the arguments made good sense. Like Raspberry, he didn't see what was such a big deal about gay marriage. How pliant moral sentiments become before the blandishments of current cultural fashions!

Over the past two decades, two major strategies emerged to deal with this situation. The first involves creating independent Catholic institutes at major American universities. The most prominent of these is the Lumen Christi Institute at the University of Chicago, but there are similar centers at other universities, e.g., the Aquinas Educational Foundation at Purdue, the Institute for Catholic Thought at the University of Illinois, the St. Anselm Institute at the University of Virginia, etc.

I sensed the unique role such an institute could play in the university when I was invited to give a lecture at the Lumen Christi Institute at the University of Chicago. The topic was Catholicism and Western culture and the lecture was held in a classroom in Swift Hall on the main quadrangle of the University. When I was a student in the

Divinity School there, I often had classes in that room, and it was a new experience to see it filled with many Catholic students and faculty (not all Catholics of course!) who had come to hear a lecture sponsored by a Catholic institute.

In that setting, I sensed a freedom about what could be said. It was possible to deal with the topic in an explicitly Catholic way and from a Catholic perspective. Yet it was still a university lecture and the audience certainly expected it to be as scholarly as other lectures given in that same room under different auspices. In fact, I knew that there would be persons in the audience who were experts on the topic and would most surely have different views than my own. A Catholic institute is no less a forum for debate and argument than the rest of the university. Catholic tradition is a living thing to be contested as well as upheld, not a genteel legacy to be perfumed and powdered.

The second major strategy has been the endowment of Catholic chairs in secular universities. Catholic chairs have been around for almost fifty years, but in recent years their number has mounted. Examples are the Arthur J. Schmitt Chair of Catholic Studies at the University of Illinois in Chicago, the William K. Warren Chair of Catholic Studies at the University of Tulsa, the Monsignor James A. Supple Chair of Catholic Studies at the Iowa State University of Iowa in Ames, and the Cottrill-Rolfes Chair in Catholic Studies at the University of Kentucky, to mention only a few.

The oldest, the Stillman Chair at Harvard University, was established in 1958 and its first incumbent was the distinguished Catholic historian, Christopher Dawson. A few years later, Yale University set up the Riggs Chair of Roman Catholic studies, and its first occupant was Stephan Kuttner, an expert in medieval canon law. Today there are several dozen Catholic chairs in universities around the country and several more are in the works.

The strongest argument for Catholic chairs is that the incumbent becomes a regular member of the university faculty and is able to offer courses for credit within a department of the university. In this setting the study and presentation of Catholicism becomes part of the academic program of the university. At its best a Catholic chair ensures that the university community has someone who can teach not only Catholic history and thought, but also address current issues from a Catholic perspective.

A limitation of Catholic chairs, however, is that whoever is appointed will probably be a specialist in history or literature or philosophy or theology, not a student of Catholicism, and will be identified as such. For example the Jesuit biblical scholar George MacRae held the Stillman chair at Harvard University for a number of years. His academic profile was less as a Catholic thinker than as a New Testament scholar. Similarly, the present incumbent at Yale University is known primarily as a historian of the 16th century and of the Reformation. It is, of course, a very good thing to have Catholic scholars of this caliber and in these areas holding Catholic chairs in major universities. But their impact on students outside their fields is limited.

In the modern university, it is easy for a Catholic chair to become another "line," that is, another faculty position serving departmental or university needs. Search committees are notorious for ignoring the obvious—why the chair was endowed in the first place. Even if the first person to hold the chair presents the Catholic tradition in its integrity and fullness, and makes a genuine effort to create a Catholic presence on campus, there is little guarantee that future occupants will have the same vision. It is seldom possible for the Church through the local bishop to have any say in the selection process. Colleges and universities are fiercely independent about faculty appointments and consider it an infringement of academic freedom to include a non-university person as part of the process of selection even in an advisory capacity.

Still, there is no reason to discourage Catholic alumni and benefactors from endowing Catholic chairs at our leading private colleges universities. Students are likely to take more seriously courses with credit offered in conjunction with other programs within the university. If Catholic parents and alumni let their universities know that it is important to have a Catholic scholar on the faculty, and donors are willing to contribute for that purpose, development officers will respond.

Nevertheless, it is shortsighted to endow Catholic chairs without an awareness of what they cannot do. Unless a Catholic chair is complemented by an independent Catholic institute, it is unlikely to awaken the interest or marshal the energies of other members of the faculty. A solitary faculty member has neither the visibility nor the resources to bring together Catholics from around the university. Nor is such an expectation likely to be part of the job description. A medievalist may seem a fine appointment—and recent decisions suggest historians may be the default preference for search committees—a specialist in the middle ages is unlikely to build bridges to faculty in the sciences, law, or medicine. And of course there is the question of which discipline or area best serves Catholic interests. The answer, of course, is that any presentation of the fullness of Catholic thought and culture requires many voices, e.g. law, history, theology, philosophy, ethics, literature, the social sciences and the natural sciences, etc.

There is a deeper question as well. Is the notion of a Catholic chair is itself a capitulation to the ideology of the secular university. Catholicism becomes an object to be studied, a social and historical phenomenon that finds it place among the myriad other phenomenon that make up the humanities and social sciences today. In announcing the appointment of a scholar for a chair in Catholic Studies at the University of California, Santa Barbara, it was stressed that Catholicism would be presented within "a comparative religious studies framework that emphasizes historical, cultural, and ethnographic approaches."

Gifted teachers and scholars can transcend the limitations imposed by the modern university, but it is more likely that they will have profiles as a historians, a sociologists, or philosophers, not as a Catholic thinkers. That is, of course, not bad. It would be a good thing if there were more courses dealing with Catholic history, philosophy, or theology. But the question is whether something more is called for.

For a genuine Catholic witness within the university it is not enough that Catholicism be presented simply as one more field of study. Yet that is the only way that the academy can welcome Catholicism. It has interest in a scholar who can teach *about* Catholicism but not someone who can speak out of the Catholic tradition as a living thing. Only the Church has such an interest. Nor can it be the business of a secular university to determine who is a fit representative of the Catholic faith. Only Catholics can decide that. A secular university that knows its own ethos and understands and respects that of the Church would not take on the burden of deciding who would be an authentic representative of the Catholic tradition.

The changing role of theology in university divinity schools over the last generation is instructive. When I was a student at the

Divinity School of the University of Chicago in the 1960s, most of the faculty were ordained Protestant ministers. Among university divinity schools, Chicago was the most liberal, linked historically to the American Baptists. Yet there was a sense among the professors that they were part of a faculty of Christian theology with responsibility to the churches as well as to the university. As the academic community has become more imperious, it filters everything through its own sieve. Divinity schools have morphed into large departments of religious studies, and their faculties have come to understand their work as the study of and teaching *about* religion. Without the presence of the Church, however formless, such a development is inevitable. As the carrier of an intellectual tradition, the Church reminds the university that that there are things worth caring about in an ultimate way, and these too have to do with the life of the mind.

When I lectured at the Lumen Christi Institute, I was no less part of the university than if I had been invited by the Divinity School or the history department, but I felt that what I had to say was not constrained by the imperious and feigned impartiality that governs so much academic discourse. I found that atmosphere liberating. At the same time I knew there were certain constraints placed on what I could say—constraints that came from the Church's teaching, from the magisterium, and my own sense of faithfulness to Catholic tradition. But these are ones that I gratefully live with in all that I do.

In the intellectual atmosphere of the modern university, it is easy for faculty and students to be cowed into thinking that judgments or convictions derived from tradition or the shared history of a religious community have no place in reasonable discourse. But there is no body of neutral knowledge just waiting to be discovered by men and women of presumed unclouded vision. Recall the quip of Robert Gascoyne-Cecil, 3rd Marquess of Salisbury: "People are fully alive to the danger of superstition in priests and in the course of time they will find out that…professors may be just as bad."

Some years ago at a faculty meeting at the University of Virginia, there was a spirited debate about whether the college of arts and sciences should approve an area elective on "moral and religious reasoning." In the discussion a prominent professor in the English department, a man of culture and learning, rose to oppose the proposal on the grounds that he did not see that religion, and, in particular,

Christianity, had anything to do with reason. In spite of his knowledge of Western culture, he had not learned what Gadamer taught us decades ago: "Reason exists for us only in concrete, historical terms."

In his lecture at Regensburg, Pope Benedict XVI argued that reason cannot be shackled by the constraints placed on it in the modern university. That was the deep truth ignored by most commentators on his address last fall. In our time, the pope said, it is assumed that reason has to do only with what can be established on empirical or mathematical grounds. Other forms of thinking are considered a matter of feeling or sentiment or faith. "In the Western world," he said, "it is widely held that only positivistic reason and the forms of philosophy based on it are universally valid." As a consequence, the scope of reason is severely reduced. But the ancient Greeks, the first teachers in our civilization, understood that one could reason about the soul, about metaphysics, about cosmology, about transcendent things and the divine, i.e., about what could not be seen or touched.

If reasoning about the soul and God, and hence about what it means to be human, is excluded from the university, the intellectual enterprise makes itself captive of the present, welcoming the past only on our terms. The dialogues of Plato will be read as works of literature not of philosophy, and the grand tradition of Christian thought will be viewed as a tribal subculture, historically instructive to be sure, but without any cognitive claim on those who study it. In that atmosphere, and that is the air that university faculty breathe today, there can be no genuine dialogue or intellectual exchange across cultures or religions. The best one can muster is: "How interesting!" For in that world our deepest convictions are seen to rest only on faith, emotion or convention, not reason or experience.

The pope reminded his academic audience of the wisdom of Socrates' words in Plato's *Phaedo*: "It would be easily understandable," said Socrates, "if someone became so annoyed at all these false notions [bandied about in the dialogue] that for the rest of his life he despised and mocked all talk about *being*— but in this way he would be deprived of the truth of existence and would suffer a great loss." To which Benedict adds: "The West has long been endangered by this aversion to the questions which underlie its rationality, and can only suffer great harm thereby. The courage to engage the whole breadth of reason, and not the denial of its grandeur—this is the programme with which a theology grounded in Biblical faith enters into the debates of our time."

In childhood Catholics come to know the Church as a community of faith and worship and service. Those who go to the university and aspire to be educated Catholics must discover that Catholicism is also a community of learning with a long history of thinking about the great questions of life. Inquiry and questioning, criticism and correction, debate and disagreement, the work of reason, are as much part of Catholicism as is the Mass, the papacy, and monastic life.

Mature faith is nurtured by thinking and the renewal of Christian culture will happen only with vigorous and imaginative intellectual leadership. Jaroslav Pelikan once wrote that the Church is not only a school, for it is also a community of prayer; but it cannot be less than a school. The valuable pastoral work of Newman centers needs to be complemented by serious Catholic scholarly institutes organized with intellectual integrity at the same level of excellence as that of the university.

At its best a Catholic institute at a university should be a kind of school within a school in which Catholic faculty and students can be apprenticed to the Catholic tradition of thought and culture. That means being introduced to a way of thinking with its own language, heroes, books, ideas, and forms of reasoning deeper and more ancient than those that dominate the modern university. It means coming to know the works of philosophers such as Josef Pieper and Jacques Maritain, poets such as Charles Péguy and Gerard Manley Hopkins, novelists such as Sigrid Undset and George Bernanos, the historian Christopher Dawson and the theologian John Courtney Murray, to invoke the name of only a few of the luminaries in the galaxy of modern Catholic writers and thinkers—and not to mention the great lights of the past. And it means making one's own the ancient maxim, "faith seeking understanding."

In *Fides et Ratio*, John Paul II wrote: "There is a profound and indissoluble unity between the knowledge of reason and the knowledge of faith. The world and all that happens within it, including history and the fate of peoples, are realities to be observed, analyzed and assessed with all the resources of reason, but without faith ever being foreign to the process." When intelligence is tested by experience, understanding informed by practice, and reason mediated by holy persons not only by ideas and arguments, reason and faith, like justice and peace in the words of the psalm, "will kiss each other."(Ps 85:10).

Professor Robert L. Wilken is the William R. Kenan, Jr., Professor of the History of Christianity at the University of Virginia in Charlottesville, Virginia. He also currently serves as the president of the St. Anselm Institute for Catholic Thought and the chairman of the board for the Center for Catholic and Evangelical Theology. Among his many publications, he lists *The Spirit of Early Christian Thought: Seeking the Face of God* (Yale University Press, 2003); *Remembering the Christian Past* (Eerdmans, 1995); and *The Land Called Holy: Palestine in Christian History and Thought* (1992).

Endnote

[1]From "An Art of Poetry" by the Australian Catholic poet, James McAuley (1917-1976).

CARDINAL WRIGHT AWARD

Remarks On Receiving
The Cardinal Wright Award

Reverend Thomas G. Weinandy, O.F.M. Cap.

I am honored to be this year's recipient of the Cardinal Wright Award. As a young seminarian I have fond memories of Cardinal Wright. He was then Bishop of Pittsburgh, and he would annually come to the St. Fidelis Seminary in Herman, Pennsylvania, to give a lecture to the staff, the seminarians and to the priests and laity in the surrounding area. I remember these talks as being timely and prophetic, some of which were on the proceedings of the Second Vatican Council which was then taking place. I remember particularly one that he gave on the horrific medical experiments performed by the Nazi doctors in the German concentration camps. The point of Cardinal Wright's talk was not that his audience should be aghast at the evils of the past but to be forewarned of the evils of the future. He said that we should not assume that our own country is immune to such horrors. Today we are well aware that what Cardinal Wright said has sadly become prophetically true. To receive an award named in the honor of such a distinguished prelate and shepherd of the Church is indeed a joy.

Moreover, since I personally know or have known so many of those who have previously received this award, I am pleased and humbled to be among their distinguished and august company. Many of the previous recipients were formative in shaping my intellectual and academic life, and even my Catholic life. I read their books and attended their lectures. What struck me then and what strikes me now is that these men and women are, as are so many members of the Fellowship of Catholic Scholars, not only highly qualified scholars, but also men and women who love the Church and the academic institutions in which they teach. They were and are consummate examples of what it means to be authentic Catholic scholars.

I want to acknowledge especially my Capuchin confrere, Father Ronald Lawler. I probably would not be receiving this award tonight if he had not been my teacher. It was he who engendered within me a love for philosophy and specifically the use of philosophy within the theological enterprise. I remember, now many years ago, when I was a college freshman and just beginning to study philosophy, Father Ronald was absent from the seminary one weekend. Being curious or better nosey students that we were, some of my classmates and I enquired about his whereabouts. We were told that he was attending a conference on metaphysics. In our ignorant arrogance we found this all quite amusing. "What," we snidely queried, "could one possibly talk about for a whole weekend when the topic was metaphysics?" Metaphysics is the study of "being" after all, and so other than acknowledging that beings do exist, what more is there to say? Little did I know then, in my juvenile conceit, how much of my academic life would be spent delving into issues metaphysical! It was indeed Father Ronald who, in the end, not only taught me just how important metaphysics is but also epistemology, and he did so by introducing me to the thought of St. Thomas Aquinas.

While I stand before you as a Franciscan, I have been from my youth, sometimes to the chagrin of my confreres, a Thomist. Given the questions and concerns that I have addressed over the years, I have found that Aquinas, on most occasions, set me on the right path even if, in the end, he did not provide me with complete answers or with answers with which I fully agreed. Nonetheless, Father Ronald, through Aquinas, introduced me not only to the metaphysical issues that philosophy properly addresses, but also, having learned to think metaphysically, I also learned to perceive the metaphysics inherent within the great Christians mysteries. It is here, over the years, that I have found my greatest intellectual and academic joy.

Even though Aquinas was most instrumental in teaching me to delve into the metaphysics of the Christian mysteries, he was not my only teacher in this regard. The Fathers of the Church and the early Councils and Creeds provided me with an abundance of wisdom and insight that are uniquely their own. Ignatius of Antioch,

Irenaeus, the great Alexandrians, Athanasius and Cyril, Leo the Great and Augustine all contributed to my understanding of the Christian mysteries, especially the mysteries of the Trinity and the Incarnation. I have spent many an hour pondering over how to conceive more clearly and articulate more accurately the metaphysics of the mysteries of the Trinity and the Incarnation. To contemplate such mysteries in the light of the Holy Spirit is to knock on the very gates of heaven and even, at times, to be permitted to peek in momentarily.

While I have probed more deeply the mysteries of the faith in the hope of obtaining a greater understanding, yet the impetus for such probing has very often been instigated by the presence of some heretical notion that spurred me into action. My doctrinal thesis was written in response to the false notion that God changes and so the Son of God changed in becoming man. However, the great fruit of that labor was not merely the refuting of an erroneous notion, but in clearly grasping the nature of God's being as pure act and the kinds of relationships that are uniquely possible for him because he is pure act. I argued that only an immutable God, who is perfectly in act, could create, and only the Son of God, as a subsistent relation fully in act, could become incarnate. Likewise, the prevailing contemporary notion that God is passible and so suffers not only allowed me to refute that misconception, but more importantly it permitted me to offer, in accordance with the Fathers of the Church and Aquinas, a positive and creative articulation of many central doctrines of the Church's faith. One of the most gratifying aspects of my final years at the University of Oxford was to know, according to the library records, that my book *Does God Suffer?* was, for two years running, the most read book of theology within the whole of the university. When one's book is, in a sense, competing with those of theologians from throughout the Christian ages, especially those written by trendy contemporaries, that statistic is rather incredible.

I have been a teacher most of my adult priestly life—at various colleges and universities as well as in adult education. As with Father Ronald, I have always believed that it is an honor and privilege to teach Catholic doctrine for one is discoursing on truths of the greatest significance—actually, they are of eternal significance. I considered the classroom as a sacred place and the lecture hour as a time of the Lord's anointing. As much as was academically allowable, I attempted to transform the lecture podium into a pulpit of evangelization, though at times I willingly let the pulpit surpass the podium and thus exceeded what was professionally permissible. Nonetheless, my joy was not merely in delineating what the Council of Nicea professed and what St. Athanasius taught, but rather observing that at least some students in the classroom were as excited about all of this as I was. I have tried, after the example of Father Ronald, to make teaching an exercise of faith—the exercise of proclaiming the faith and the exercise of eliciting of faith from those who hear the proclamation.

While I was very reluctant to leave Oxford, since the Lord had blessed so much of what I did there, I concluded that it would be good for me to take up my present position at the United States Conference of Catholic Bishops. One friend of mine, who is also a good friend of Father Ronald's, suggested to me that, since the offer to work for the bishops came shortly after Father Ronald died, he was very much involved in this offer being made. I said to this person that that thought had already crossed my mind. Whether Father Ronald was orchestrating events from heaven is not the real point. The point is that Father Ronald loved the Church and he knew that I was striving to love the Church as he did. It was this love for the Church that compelled Father Ronald to do so much of what he did and it is that same love for the Church that ultimately compelled me to leave my beloved Oxford for the USCCB. My present work is not, on the whole, a high adrenalin job. It does not provide the same emotional delight and intellectual satisfaction of the lecture room and the academy, but it is an important job that does serve the bishops in a very unique and critical manner. In undertaking it, I serve the Church as a whole within the United States, and that in itself is no small distinction that provides much gratification and joy. Of course, to a few people some of what I am about is so important that, as you are probably well aware, it actually gets leaked to the press. In our media crazed world of today, one knows that one has made the "big time" when one is compelled to say to the press: "Because of the sensitivity of the issue, I have no comment."

The life that I have lived thus far as a Capuchin priest is not the life I thought I would live as I progressed through the seminary. Nonetheless, I have enjoyed all of its various twists and turns. I have been especially fortunate, within all of the pastoral and academic ministries, in coming to know many men and women of profound faith, such as you within the Fellowship. In my present position I have come to work with many faithful bishops who are admirable shepherds and teachers, and my present staff members are exemplary in their faith and commendable in their professionalism. It is this sustaining fellowship of faith that has supported and sustained me in my striving to profess the Gospel in and out of season. Again, I want to thank the Fellowship of Catholic Scholars for honoring me with the Cardinal Wright Award. I pray, and I ask you to pray, that I might always be faithful to that for which it stands—fidelity to the Gospel as professed by the Catholic Church to the glory of Jesus Christ our Lord. Thank you.

Father Thomas G. Weinandy, O.F.M., Cap., has since January, 2005, been Executive Director of the Secretariat for Doctrine and Pastoral Practices of the United States Conference of Catholic Bishops in Washington, D.C. He was ordained to the priesthood in 1972. He holds a doctorate in historical theology from King's College, University of London. His major fields of specialization are Christology, Trinitarian theology, Soteriology, and the philosophy of God. He has taught at Georgetown University, Mount St. Mary's University in Emmitsburg, Maryland, the Franciscan University of Steubenville, Loyola College, and Oxford University. His books include *Aquinas on Scripture* (2005); *Aquinas on Doctrine* (2004); *The Theology of St. Cyril of Alexandria* (2003); *Does God Suffer?* (2000); *The Sacrament of Mercy* (1997); and *The Father's Spirit of Sonship* (1995). He has also written numerous articles, popular and scholarly, in such publications as *New Covenant, National Catholic Register, Pastoral Life, Canadian Catholic Review, New Oxford Review, Arlington Catholic Herald*, and *The Family*.

APPENDIX

Fellowship of Catholic Scholars

Membership Information

For information about joining the Fellowship of Catholic Scholars, visit our website at www.catholicscholars.org, or contact the Executive Secretary, the Rev. Msgr. Stuart Swetland at:

Rev. Msgr. Stuart Swetland, S.T.D.
Executive Secretary, Fellowship of Catholic Scholars
c/o Mt. St. Mary's University
16300 Old Emmitsburg Road
Emmitsburg, MD 21727

TEL: 301-447-3453

E-MAIL: swetland@msmary.edu

For questions regarding: 1) joining the Fellowship; 2) changing your address or biographical information; or the Fellowship Web Page, you may contact:

James Shank
604 E. Armory Avenue
Champaign, Illinois 61820
TEL: 217-255-6625
E-MAIL: james.shank@sjcnc.org
OR: visit the FCS website at:
www.catholicscholars.org

Statement of Purpose

1. We, Catholic scholars in various disciplines, join in fellowship in order to serve Jesus Christ better, by helping one another in our work and by putting our abilities more fully at the service of the Catholic faith.

2. We wish to form a Fellowship of Catholic Scholars who see their intellectual work as expressing the service they owe to God. To Him we give thanks for our Catholic faith and for every opportunity He gives us to serve that faith

3. We wish to form a Fellowship of Catholic Scholars open to the work of the Holy Spirit within the Church. Thus we wholeheartedly accept and support the renewal of the Church of Christ undertaken by Pope John XXIII, shaped by Vatican Council II, and carried on by succeeding popes.

4. We accept as the rule of our life and thought the entire faith of the Catholic Church. This we see not merely in solemn definitions but in the ordinary teaching of the pope and the bishops in union with him, and also embodied in those modes of worship and ways of Christian life, of the present as of the past, which have been in harmony with the teaching of St. Peter's successors in the See of Rome.

5. The questions raised by contemporary thought must be considered with courage and dealt with in honesty. We will seek to do this, faithful to the truth always guarded in the Church by the Holy Spirit, and sensitive to the needs of the family of faith. We wish to accept a responsibility which a Catholic scholar may not evade: to assist everyone, so far as we are able, to personal assent to the mystery of Christ as made manifest through the lived faith of the Church, His Body, and through the active charity without which faith is dead.

6. To contribute to this sacred work, our Fellowship will strive to:
    *   Come to know and welcome all who share our purpose;
    *   Make known to one another our various competencies and interests;
    *   Share our abilities with one another unstintingly in

our efforts directed to our common purpose;
- Cooperate in clarifying the challenges which must be met;
- Help one another to evaluate critically the variety of responses which are proposed to these challenges;
- Communicate our suggestions and evaluations to members of the Church who might find them helpful;
- Respond to requests to help the Church in her work of guarding the faith as inviolable and defending it with fidelity;
- Help one another to work through, in scholarly and prayerful fashion and without public dissent, any problem which may arise from magisterial teaching.

7. With the grace of God for which we pray, we hope to assist the whole Church to understand her own identity more clearly, to proclaim the joyous Gospel of Jesus more confidently, and to carry out it redemptive work to all humankind more effectively.

Member Benefits

All members receive four issues annually of the *The Fellowship of Catholic Scholars Quarterly*, which includes scholarly articles, important documentation, book reviews, news, and occasional Fellowship symposia.

All members are invited to attend the annual FCS convention held in various cities where, by custom, the local ordinary greets and typically celebrates Mass for the members of the Fellowship. The typical convention program includes: Daily Mass; Keynote Address; at least six scholarly sessions with speakers who are customarily invited to help develop and illustrate the theme of each convention chosen by the FCS Board of Directors; a Banquet and Reception with Awards; and a membership business meeting and occasional substantive meetings devoted to subjects of current interest in the Church.

Current members receive a copy of the "Proceedings" of each convention, consisting of an attractive volume with the title of the convention theme and containing the texts of the conventions speeches and other material of interest to the membership. Every three or four years all members receive a Membership Directory with current information on Fellowship members (addresses, telephone numbers, faxes, e-mails, etc.).

National Awards

The Fellowship grants the following Awards, usually presented during the annual convention:

The Cardinal Wright Award – Presented annually to a Catholic judged to have done outstanding service for the Church in the tradition of the late Cardinal John J. Wright, former Bishop of Pittsburgh and later Prefect for the Congregation for the Clergy in Rome. The recipients of this Award have been:

1979 – Rev. Msgr. George A. Kelly
1980 – Dr. William E. May
1981 – Dr. James F. Hitchcock
1982 – Dr. Germain Grisez
1983 – Rev. John Connery, S.J.
1984 – Rev. John A. Hardon, S.J.
1985 – Herbert Ratner, M.D.
1986 – Dr. Joseph P. Scottino
1987 – Rev. Joseph Farraher, & Rev. Joseph Fessio, S.J.
1988 – Rev. John F. Harvey, O.S.F.S.
1989 – Dr. John Finnis
1990 – Rev. Ronald Lawler, O.F.M. Cap.
1991 – Rev. Francis Canavan, S.J.
1992 – Rev. Donald J. Keefe, S.J.
1993 – Dr. Janet E. Smith
1994 – Dr. Jude P. Dougherty
1995 – Rev. Msgr. William B. Smith
1996 – Dr. Ralph McInerny
1997 – Rev. James V. Schall, S.J.
1998 – Rev. Msgr. Michael J. Wrenn &
         Kenneth D. Whitehead
1999 – Dr. Robert P. George

2000 – Dr. Mary Ann Glendon
2001 – Thomas W. Hilgers, M.D.
2002 – Rev. J. Augustine DiNoia, O.P.
2003 – Prof. Elizabeth Fox-Genovese
2004 – Sr. Mary Prudence Allen, R.S.M.
2005 – Prof. Gerard V. Bradley
2006 – Dr. Patrick Lee
2007 – Fr. Thomas G. Weinandy, O.F.M. Cap.

The Cardinal O'Boyle Award – This Award is given occasionally to individuals whose actions demonstrate a courage and witness in favor of the Catholic Faith similar to that exhibited by the late Cardinal Patrick A. O'Boyle, Archbishop of Washington, in the face of the pressures of contemporary society which tend to undermine the faith. The recipients of this award have been:
　　1988 – Rev. John C. Ford, S.J.
　　1991 – Mother Angelica, P.C.P.A., EWTN
　　1995 – John and Sheila Kippley, Couple to Couple League
　　1997 – Rep. Henry J. Hyde (R.-IL)
　　2002 – Senator Rick Santorum (R.-PA)
　　2003 – Secretary of Housing and Urban Development, the
　　　　　　Honorable Melquiades R. Martinez
　　　　　　(later U.S. senator from Florida) and
　　　　　　　Mrs. Kathryn Tindal Martinez
　　2004 – Rep. Christopher J. Smith (R.-NJ) and Marie Smith
　　2005 – Helen Hull Hitchcock
　　2006 – Senator Samuel D. Brownback (R.-KS)
　　2007 – Peggy Hartshorn, Ph.D., Heartbeat International

The Founder's Award – Given occasionally to individuals with a record of outstanding service in defense of the Catholic faith and in support of the Catholic intellectual life. In 2002, the Award was presented to Fr. Joseph Fessio, S.J., in 2003, to Fr. Ronald Lawler, O.F.M.Cap., and in 2007, to Professor Ralph McInerny

Presidents of the Fellowship of Catholic Scholars
2004 -　　　Dean Bernard Dobranski, Ave Maria Law School
2003 – 2004　Prof. Gerard V. Bradley, Notre Dame Law School

2002 – 2003   Dean Bernard Dobranski, Ave Maria Law School
2001 – 2002   Rev. Thomas F. Dailey, O.S.F.S., DeSales University
1995 – 2001   Prof. Gerard V. Bradley, Notre Dame Law School
1991 – 1995   Prof. Ralph McInerny, University of Notre Dame
1989 – 1991   Rev. Kenneth Baker, S.J., Editor,
              Homiletic & Pastoral Review
1987 – 1989   Prof. William E. May, John Paul II Institute on
              Marriage and the Family
1985 – 1987   Rev. Msgr. George A. Kelly, St. John's University
1983 – 1985   Rev. Earl Weiss, S.J., Loyola University
1981 – 1983   Rev. Msgr. William B. Smith, St. Joseph's Seminary
1979 – 1981   Prof. James F. Hitchcock, St. Louis University
1977 – 1979   Rev. Ronald Lawler, O.F.M.Cap., Diocese of
              Pittsburgh